CHARLES F. STANLEY BIBLE STUDY SERIES

PRACTICING BASIC SPIRITUAL DISCIPLINES

FOLLOW GOD'S BLUEPRINT FOR LIVING

CHARLES F. STANLEY

THOMAS NELSON
Since 1798

PRACTICING BASIC SPIRITUAL DISCIPLINES
CHARLES F. STANLEY BIBLE STUDY SERIES

Copyright © 1996, 2009, 2020 by Charles F. Stanley.

Published in Nashville, Tennessee, by Thomas Nelson. Thomas Nelson is a registered trademark of HarperCollins Christian Publishing, Inc.

All Scripture quotations are taken from the New King James Version.® Copyright © 1982 by Thomas Nelson. Used by permission. All rights reserved worldwide.

Thomas Nelson titles may be purchased in bulk for educational, business, fundraising, or sales promotional use. For information, e-mail SpecialMarkets@ThomasNelson.com.

ISBN 978-0-310-10570-1 (softcover)
ISBN 978-0-310-10595-4 (ebook)

First Printing August 2020 / Printed in the United States of America
HB 01.12.2024

CONTENTS

OUR BLUEPRINT FOR STRENGTH

Every building begins with a blueprint. If the engineering is faulty on the blueprint, the resulting structure will be weak. The same is true when it comes to our spiritual lives. The strength of our faith in Christ rests first and foremost on the absolute reliability and truth of God's Word.

Thank God that we have a blueprint for spiritual strength that does not fail! We can rely on the Bible as our blueprint for living with *complete confidence*. It gives us God's truth and tells us how to apply that truth. It is a book of genuine wisdom about how to become strong spiritually... and how to stay that way. Just as builders return to blueprints often during the construction of a structure, so we must return to the Bible often during the development of our spiritual lives. As we do, we make certain we are staying on track in our spiritual growth.

This book can be used by you alone or by several people in a small-group study. At various times, you will be asked to relate to the material in one of the following four ways.

First, what new insights have you gained? Make notes about the insights you have. You may want to record them in your Bible or in a separate journal. As you reflect on your new understanding, you are likely to see how God has moved in your life.

Second, have you ever had a similar experience? You approach the Bible from your own unique background... your own particular set of understandings about the world that you bring with you when you open God's Word. For this reason, it is important to consider how your experiences are shaping your understanding and allow yourself to be open to the truth that God reveals.

Third, how do you feel about the material? While you should not depend solely on your emotions as a gauge for your faith, it is important for you to be aware of them as you study a passage of Scripture and can freely express them to God. Sometimes, the Holy Spirit will use your emotions to compel you to look at your life in a different or challenging way.

Fourth, in what way do you feel challenged to respond or to act? God's Word may inspire you or challenge you to take a particular action. Take this challenge seriously and find ways to move into it. If God reveals a particular need that He wants you to address, take that as His "marching orders." God will empower you to do something with the challenge that He has just given you.

Start your Bible study sessions in prayer. Ask God to give you spiritual eyes to see and spiritual ears to hear. As you conclude your study, ask the Lord to seal what you have learned so you will not forget it. Ask Him to help you grow into the fullness of the nature and character of Christ Jesus.

I encourage you to keep the Bible at the center of your study. A genuine Bible study stays focused on God's Word and promotes a growing faith and a closer walk with the Holy Spirit in each person who participates.

Preparing for Spiritual Growth

IN THIS LESSON

Learning: How do I prepare myself to grow spiritually?

Growing: What steps can I take to examine myself before I seek to grow in the spiritual disciplines?

Do you know what all children have in common, regardless of what differences there may be in terms of culture, time, and geography? The answer is *growth*. It doesn't matter where children are or what age they are—they all grow. In fact, lack of growth is one of the ways that doctors know something is wrong with a child in terms of his or her development.

The same is true for children of God. When we are saved through faith in Jesus Christ, our lives should be marked by spiritual growth from that moment forward. The apostle Paul said that we will no longer live as spiritual children but will "grow up in all things into Him who is the head—Christ" (Ephesians 4:15). In the same manner, Peter commanded Christians to "desire the pure milk of the word, that you may grow thereby" (1 Peter 2:2).

To live as a Christian means to grow spiritually each day so we move closer to Christ with every season of our lives. Spiritual growth is a natural process for every follower of Christ. Of course, we know that things don't always go as they *should* go. Sometimes things get off kilter. This can certainly happen with our spiritual lives.

So, what should we do when we encounter seasons where our spiritual growth seems stunted or stagnant? How should we respond when we don't appear to be growing closer to Jesus in our lives—when those old patterns and old habits keep popping up? What should we do when it feels we have lost all our spiritual momentum?

SPIRITUAL DISCIPLINES AND SPIRITUAL GROWTH

Spiritual disciplines are one of the biggest factors that contribute to spiritual growth. Think about this in terms of new believers. When people come to Christ, they tend to grow quickly (and noticeably) in their spiritual lives because they start spending time in the Word of God, praying, attending church, and connecting with other believers. This growth comes about because they are engaging in these spiritual disciplines.

In this study, we will explore basic spiritual disciplines because they are critical not only for new Christians but also for *everyone* who chooses to follow Christ. In the sessions to come, we will explore how to strengthen personal study of Scripture, how to give faithfully, what it means to connect with God, and more. We will examine these core spiritual disciplines and how they apply to our lives—regardless of our level of experience as followers of Christ.

However, I want to start in this lesson by exploring something different. I have found it is possible for Christians to practice the spiritual disciplines and not experience growth because they are just going through the motions. Our hearts must be connected to our actions. So, we first need to examine our spiritual lives in a meaning-ful way. More accurately, we need to ask *God* to examine our hearts and reveal anything that may be blocking our spiritual growth.

I know from experience this process requires effort on our part. But I promise it will be worth it. When we work with God to examine our spiritual lives, we gain a keen sense of what we need to do to move forward and to mature spiritually the way the Lord intended. We will then be ready to supercharge that growth by practicing the basic spir-itual disciplines.

1. Are you currently in a season of spiritual growth or spiritual stag-nation? Explain.

2. What are you hoping to learn or experience throughout this study? Why?

ALLOW GOD TO EXAMINE YOUR HEART

Psalm 139 has long been recognized as one of David's most beautiful psalms. It's a work of art, and it begins with a poignant reality: "O LORD, You have searched me and known me. You know my sitting down and my rising up; You understand my thought afar off. You comprehend my path and my lying down, and are acquainted with all my ways" (verses 1–3).

David started this magnificent poem by acknowledging that God knew him inside and out. There wasn't a thought or an action in David's life that God did not see and understand. Of course, the same is true for us as followers of Jesus today. God knows everything about us. He is all-knowing. This knowledge penetrates even to the most personal aspects of our lives.

That being the case, the final two verses of Psalm 139 are especially interesting: "Search me, O God, and know my heart; Try me, and know my anxieties; and see if *there is any* wicked way in me, and lead me in the way everlasting" (verses 23–24). David was requesting a personal encounter with God. He was saying, *"Lord, I want you to scan my life. I'm ready for some spiritual surgery. Help me see myself the way You see me. Leave nothing unexposed."*

David intended this examination to cover his entire life. He wanted God to "search" both his actions and his attitudes. He wanted God to test his heart—his "anxieties." He wanted God to highlight anything that might be "wicked" inside him. He desired God to lead him "in the way everlasting." In other words, he wanted to continue growing spiritually. He wanted to truly know himself so he could make significant progress in connecting more deeply with God.

This is a crucial step for all Christians. If we want to experience spiritual growth—especially if we want to maximize our growth through the spiritual disciplines—we need to get an accurate picture of our spiritual lives. We need to pray, *"Lord, look at me through the lens of Your all-knowing eyes. Show me anything that doesn't belong in my life.*

Show me anything that is preventing me from growing in my spiritual relationship with You."

3. What do you like best about David's request in Psalm 139?

....

....

....

....

....

....

....

....

....

4. What emotions do you experience when you think about asking God to examine or evaluate your life?

....

....

....

....

....

....

....

BE HONEST WITH YOURSELF

Asking God to examine and evaluate us in this manner will require a lot from us. It is not just wishful thinking. It will require us first and foremost to be willing to look inside our own minds and our own hearts—even if we don't like what we find there. It will require *honesty.* We need to be honest with ourselves if we want to gain anything from the experience.

Why is this? Because it is easy to blame others for our faults or the different ways we go astray. It is easy for us to say, "God, there may be a problem here, but You need to understand it is not my fault. This person did this to me when I was young—or that person did that to me when I was older—and that is why I do the things I do."

Remember the first thing David emphasized in Psalm 139: *God's omniscience*. The Lord knows all things, which means He knows everything about us. Because this is true, there is simply no use in trying to hide from God or deflect the truth about our own hearts. He already knows. We cannot fool Him. When we are dishonest about what the Holy Spirit reveals, we don't have a shot at fixing things. We don't have a chance of getting better.

5. When has God revealed something uncomfortable to you about yourself? What happened next?

6. What obstacles tend to prevent you from being honest about your own life?

REALIZE THE PROCESS INVOLVES TIME

The process of examining ourselves—of asking God to search us and reveal what He finds—is a *process*. It is not something that just happens in a moment and is done. It requires time. The reason is because God loves us enough to not expose the reality of who we are in one moment.

If most people were to get an accurate view of the lives they have led and who they really are inside, it would be so distasteful, hurtful, and painful to them that they could hardly stand it. Instead of helping them, the revelation would be so terrible that it might compel them to turn to alcohol, drugs, or other unhealthy behaviors to bury the pain.

It takes time to really know yourself. Consider this: you didn't grow up overnight. Every single day of your life has added something to who you are. Every day has added to the emotions you have experienced, the thoughts you have entertained, and the choices you have made. So, when you ask God to reveal who you truly are, He starts slowly. He gives you a little bit at first—something you can handle. Then, over time, He reveals more and more. He goes deeper and deeper until He brings you to a place where you are ready and able to move forward.

I am sure that you have experienced tremendous hurt in your life. You have gone through pain, rejection, loss, unforgiveness, bitterness, resentment, and hostility. Maybe all at the same time. You have been hurt in many different ways. Therefore, God takes it slowly when it comes to revealing the sources and the consequences of that hurt. He peels things away one layer at a time so you are not overwhelmed by everything being exposed at once.

David said, "Try me, and know my anxieties" (Psalm 139:23). It won't happen quickly. So, as you prepare to examine yourself, be ready to invest as much time as God requires to help you get an accurate picture of where you are and where you need to go.

7. How much time do you give to God in prayer during a given day? In a given week?

....

....

....

....

....

....

8. Where can you set aside time this week specifically for this process of examining yourself through God's eyes?

....

....

....

....

....

....

BE COURAGEOUS

Let me remind you of the case I am making in this lesson. Namely, you will never be the person God wants you to be until you let Him show you the person you are. It doesn't matter how methodically or mechanically you practice the spiritual disciplines. You first need to get an accurate picture of yourself before those disciplines will accomplish anything in your life.

Take it from me . . . that will require courage. There was a time in my life when everything seemed good. I was a young pastor with a young family. On the outside, everything was working well. However, on the inside, I knew something wasn't right. I wasn't experiencing my connection with God the way I was used to experiencing it.

I wasn't growing spiritually the way that I wanted to grow. There was a problem, but I didn't know what it was.

So, I prayed a prayer like the one David recorded in Psalm 139. *"Lord, show me what's wrong. Show me what's blocking my connection with You."* In response, God opened my eyes to see a part of my heart I had never fully considered—and it scared me. It made me want to clam up and not go any farther down that road of self-examination.

Specifically, God showed me the poison I had allowed into my life because of bitterness against my stepfather. My father died when I was nine months old, and my mother did not remarry until I was nine years old. When she did remarry, there was a lot of conflict between my stepfather and me. Lots of tension. I felt he was unkind and ugly toward my mother. It created a lot of resentment and hostility in my heart toward him.

When God revealed this to me, I chose not to do anything about it for several months. I put the whole thing out of my mind . . . or at least I attempted to do so. But every time I would take my place behind the pulpit to preach, it was as if I could see my stepfather sitting right there in the front row. I could not escape what God had showed to me.

So, eventually, I went to see my stepfather. When I sat down across a table from him, I told him openly and honestly what God had revealed. I spoke about what I felt and why I felt it. I then did something that required courage: I asked my stepfather to forgive me for the bitterness, anger, resentment, and hostility I had stored up inside my heart for all those years.

Now, this did not mean that I accepted everything that he had done in the past. Nor did it mean I was condoning his actions for all those years growing up. No, I simply apologized for what I had allowed into my heart—my thoughts and my emotions I had stored up against him.

When I walked out of his house, it was as if God had pulled the plug on the emotional blockage inside me. And not just an emotional blockage—but a spiritual blockage as well. In fact, I can look back on that time and see it was after that moment I began to grow and connect with God in a way I had never before experienced. My understanding of God and my relationship with Him increased dramatically, and God began to do things in my life and through my life that I had never dreamed were possible.

So, I want to tell you that truly examining yourself will require courage. It will not be easy. But it will be worth it. The rewards will be incredible, because you will grow spiritually. It will be the key to unlocking a more intimate connection with God—and it will be a critical step in maximizing everything God wants you to experience through the spiritual disciplines.

9. Do you consider yourself to be a person of courage? Why or why not?

....

....

....

....

....

....

....

10. What are you most afraid of discovering if you examine yourself the way David described?

....

....

....

....

....

....

....

TODAY AND TOMORROW

Today: I will not become the person God created me to be until I truly understand who I am now.

Tomorrow: I will examine myself with honesty and courage so that I can experience true spiritual growth.

CLOSING PRAYER

Father, how grateful we are that Your love never changes. It is not prejudiced. It is not forgetful. It is always the same. You are always ready to hear our confession and the cry of our hearts. Today, we ask that You would examine our hearts. Look at us through the lens of Your all-knowing eyes. Reveal anything that is unhealthy that does not belong there. We are willing to change, and we thank You for revealing Your truths to us. In Jesus' name we pray. Amen.

Notes and Prayer Requests

Use this space to write any key points, questions, or prayer requests from this week's study.

THE STRENGTH OF THE BELIEVER

IN THIS LESSON

Learning: What does it mean to be spiritually strong?

Growing: How can I remain consistently strong?

Of one thing we can be certain today: The Lord wants our faith as Christians to be rock-solid. At no time do we find God calling His people to be weak in spiritual power, wavering in purpose, or wandering aimlessly through life. We are called to be strong in faith, certain of our salvation, and sure of our direction and eternal destiny.

The Bible describes the Lord as a rock. David said this in a praise song to the Lord: "I will love You, O LORD, my strength. The LORD is my rock and my fortress and my deliverer; my God, my strength, in whom I will trust" (Psalm 18:1-2). Elsewhere, David refers to the

Lord as the source of his strength: "In God is my salvation and my glory; the rock of my strength, and my refuge, is in God" (62:7). He describes God as the foundation of his salvation: "He shall cry to Me, 'You are my Father, My God, and the rock of my salvation'" (89:26). He states the Lord is his steadfast defense: "The Lord has been my defense, and my God the rock of my refuge" (94:22). David viewed God as a sure foundation—an immovable and impenetrable fortress.

In the New Testament, we find Jesus referred to as our spiritual Rock. As Paul wrote, "Brethren, I do not want you to be unaware that all our fathers were under the cloud, all passed through the sea, all were baptized into Moses in the cloud and in the sea, all ate the same spiritual food, and all drank the same spiritual drink. For they drank of that spiritual Rock that followed them, and that Rock was Christ" (1 Corinthians 10:1–4). Paul also described Jesus as the "chief cornerstone" on which the entire church has been built (Ephesians 2:20).

1. "I will say of the LORD, 'He is my refuge and my fortress; my God, in Him I will trust'" (Psalm 91:2). How has God been a refuge and fortress for you in times of need?

....

....

....

....

....

....

....

....

2. "Now, therefore, you are no longer strangers and foreigners, but fellow citizens with the saints and members of the household of God, having been built on the foundation of the apostles and

prophets, Jesus Christ Himself being the chief cornerstone" (Ephesians 2:19-20). What does it mean that Jesus is the chief cornerstone of the church?

....

....

....

....

....

....

....

STAND STRONG IN YOUR CONVICTIONS

When we trust Jesus Christ to be our Savior and Lord, we are placing ourselves on a firm foundation that never falters and never fails. We are placing ourselves on a foundation that does not shift, crumble, or crack. We are placing ourselves on a foundation that is eternal and unchanging. We become part of God's holy and living temple— a "dwelling place of God in the Spirit"—and as such we are to bear the same qualities as the foundation on which we are built (Ephesians 2:21-22). We remain strong in times of crisis or persecution, solid in our understanding of the Scriptures, sure of our relationship with God, and steadfast in our pursuit of all that the Holy Spirit calls us to. We are like boulders in a world of shifting sands.

Although the world says that black is white and white is black, that morals don't matter, and that all things are relative, we are to stand strong as Christians. We are to clearly discern right from wrong, good from bad, and the eternal from the temporary. The world calls us to do what feels good and justifies behavior under the banner of "everybody is doing it," but we are to stand strong as Christians and declare that our behavior is rooted in our faith, not our emotions. Even if everybody around us bows to the false gods of this age, we will not bow.

In the book of Daniel, we read the story of three Hebrew young men who had to take such a stand. At the time, the people of Judah were being held in captivity by the Babylonians. The Babylonian king, a man named Nebuchadnezzar, determined one day to commission a grand statue of himself to be made out of gold. He then issued an edict requiring all people living in his realm to bow down at an appointed time and worship his image.

Failure to comply would result in dire consequences. As the king's herald announced: "To you it is commanded, O peoples, nations, and languages, that at the time you hear the sound of the horn . . . you shall fall down and worship the gold image that King Nebuchadnezzar has set up; and whoever does not fall down and worship shall be cast immediately into the midst of a burning fiery furnace" (Daniel 3:4–6). But the three Hebrew young men refused to bow down. They said to the king, "Let it be known to you, O king, that we do not serve your gods, nor will we worship the gold image which you have set up" (verse 18).

In a rage, Nebuchadnezzar ordered the men to be thrown into the fiery furnace. But the Lord spared them from the flames. When they stepped out, "the hair of their head was not singed nor were their garments affected, and the smell of fire was not on them" (verse 27).

The world often calls us to reject God's commandments as old-fashioned or out of touch. But we are to remember the example of these three young men and stand strong. God does not change, and His commandments are as applicable today as they were in biblical times. He remains in touch with the human heart and with human need. The world calls us to do what is politically correct, economically expedient, and morally compromising, but we are to stand strong as Christians and choose to be God's people, generous in helping the needy, pure in our hearts, and uncompromising in our belief that God is sovereign.

3. "Our God whom we serve is able to deliver us from the burning fiery furnace, and He will deliver us from your hand, O king. But if not . . . we [will not] worship the gold image which you have set up" (Daniel 3:17–18). What do these verses say about the strength the three young men had to stand up for their convictions?

....

....

....

....

....

....

4. When is a time that you had to take a difficult stand for your Christian convictions?

....

....

....

....

....

....

....

PURSUE GODLY STRENGTH

Athletes know that they must do certain things to become strong. They must eat foods that build up their bodies physically. They must exercise in ways that produce strength, flexibility, and endurance. They must also get sufficient rest for the renewal of their muscles. There is a *discipline* required of those who desire to become good athletes. The higher the level of performance the athlete seeks, the greater the discipline required to reach it.

The same is true for each of us in our spiritual walk. If we are going to be strong in the faith, we must follow a spiritual discipline.

We must take into our lives those things that produce strength in us and eliminate those things that result in weakness, laziness, or spiritual compromise. We must exercise our spiritual muscles by using our faith in ways that promote the spread of the gospel, strengthen the body of Christ, and meet the physical and spiritual needs we encounter. If we want to succeed in our spiritual growth, we must learn to rest in the Lord, trusting Him always to provide for us and protect us against the enemy of our souls.

The apostle Paul stated it this way: "Do you not know that those who run in a race all run, but one receives the prize? Run in such a way that you may obtain it. And everyone who competes for the prize is temperate in all things. Now they do it to obtain a perishable crown, but we for an imperishable crown. Therefore I run thus: not with uncertainty. Thus I fight: not as one who beats the air. But I discipline my body and bring it into subjection, lest, when I have preached to others, I myself should become disqualified" (1 Corinthians 9:24–27).

The Christian life cannot be lived on a whim, following fad beliefs. It must be a life of consistent, daily discipline. As Paul also challenged the Philippians, "Let your conduct be worthy of the gospel of Christ" (Philippians 1:27). That must always be our goal.

5. "Bodily exercise profits a little, but godliness is profitable for all things, having promise of the life that now is and of that which is to come" (1 Timothy 4:8). What are the similarities between physical exercise and spiritual exercise?

6. Why do you think Paul says spiritual exercise (pursuing godliness) is more beneficial? How have you seen the truth of this in your own life?

....

....

....

....

....

....

LEAD A LIFE OF CONSISTENCY

As a pastor, I have asked countless people, "How are you doing?" I tend to receive these replies: "Oh, I'm having my ups and downs." "Well, I'm going through a wilderness time right now." "I'm just trying to stay on top of things." Some have admitted, "I'm not as close to God as I should be," or even, "I've been away from the Lord but I'm on my way back."

These statements all suggest that most Christians do not live the *consistently strong* spiritual life they desire and know God wants them to live. They are riding the rollercoaster of life rather than walking a steady, upward path. When I have asked, "What are you doing to be strong spiritually?" I have heard a variety of answers, but I often receive a response that means, "I don't know what to do." Many have never imagined that it is possible to live a *consistently strong* spiritual life. They take ups and downs for granted and even expect them.

That is not what the Lord desires for us. Paul said to the Colossians, "I am with you in spirit, rejoicing to see your good order and the steadfastness of your faith in Christ. As you therefore have received Christ Jesus the Lord, so walk in Him, rooted and built up in Him and established in the faith, as you have been taught, abounding in it with thanksgiving" (Colossians 2:5–7). Paul also assured the Colossians that they would be considered "holy, and blameless, and above reproach" if they would "continue in the faith, grounded and steadfast, and [not be] moved away from the hope of the gospel" (1:22–23).

In a similar manner, Paul instructed the Ephesians, "Be strong in the Lord and in the power of His might. Put on the whole armor of God, that you may be able to stand against the wiles of the devil. For we do not wrestle against flesh and blood, but against principalities, against powers, against the rulers of the darkness of this age, against spiritual hosts of wickedness in the heavenly places. Therefore take up the whole armor of God, that you may be able to withstand in the evil day, and having done all, to stand" (Ephesians 6:10–13).

Notice Paul's instruction to put on the *whole armor of God*. This is a daily practice. Each day, we must consistently "suit up" so that we can stand strong against our enemy.

7. "Therefore, my beloved brethren, be steadfast, immovable, always abounding in the work of the Lord, knowing that your labor is not in vain in the Lord" (1 Corinthians 15:58). Why is it important to be consistent in practicing daily spiritual disciplines?

8. What are some of the main challenges you face in being consistent in practicing spiritual disciplines (such as spending time in prayer or reading the Bible)?

Practice Spiritual Disciplines

At the outset of this study, I asked you if you would consider yourself a *growing* Christian. As Peter instructed, you are to "desire the pure milk of the word, that you may grow thereby" (1 Peter 2:2). In the original Greek, the word *grow* is a present active imperative tense of the verb, which means "to grow and keep growing" and "to advance and keep advancing." It is something that is to be continually taking place in your life.

Now, this doesn't mean that you are going to grow equally every single day, or every single week, or even every single month. But it does mean that you are experiencing growth over time. There is none of this stagnation and loss of interest in the things of God. You recognize that God is continuing to do something amazing in your life.

So, what do you need to do to reach this state where you are strong and *remain* strong in your spirit? How are you to discipline your life to be consistent and unwavering in your walk of faith? The elements of a disciplined life in Christ are the subject of this Bible study. As you read through these lessons, let me encourage you on the following three points.

First, the foundation of the spiritual disciplines is the same whether you are a newborn babe in Christ—newly saved—or a longtime Christian. You will never outgrow your need for the basics of spiritual discipline. You will never outgrow your need for God's Word, your need to pray, your need to follow God's command to give, your need for Christian fellowship, or your need to obey God's call to ministry. No person is so spiritually mature that he or she can just ignore the basics and still expect to remain strong over time.

Second, the foundation of the spiritual disciplines is the same regardless of your personal circumstances. Pastors and laymen need to pursue the same basic spiritual disciplines to be strong in the Lord.

Everyone—men and women, rich and poor, young and old, highly educated and uneducated—needs the same basic spiritual disciplines. If you choose not to feed on the Word of God, you are simply going to stagnate in your Christian life. There are no exceptions. It doesn't make any difference how many sermons a person has preached, or how many seminaries that person has attended, or how many PhDs or ThDs or whatever other titles are behind his or her name. If you do not read the Word of God, you will stagnate in your spiritual walk. This will be devastating to your Christian life and to your Christian testimony.

Third, the call to practice the spiritual disciplines is a call for everyone. I once met a person who said to me, "I'm just not as spiritual as some people. I just tend to struggle more than others." The fact is that we *all* struggle to remain consistent in our spiritual lives. However, God has given each of us the will necessary to pursue a disciplined spiritual life and also the power of the Holy Spirit to help us remain strong and consistent in our spiritual walk. Our will, plus the Holy Spirit's power, is true willpower. *Every person* can become spiritually disciplined.

9. "Therefore let him who thinks he stands take heed lest he fall" (1 Corinthians 10:12). What is the danger in believing that you are so spiritually "mature" that you can skip or choose not to engage in spiritual discipline?

10. In what areas do you need God to give you the will to pursue a disciplined spiritual life?

....

....

....

....

....

....

....

....

TODAY AND TOMORROW

Today: The Lord gives me His Holy Spirit's power to
enable me to be strong.

Tomorrow: I will spend time this week working on
regular spiritual disciplines.

CLOSING PRAYER

*Heavenly Father, we declare today that You are our refuge and our strength.
We commit today to trust only in You and not in the things of this world.
We thank You for not only giving us eternal life but also for the exciting, ongoing, and challenging experience of growing in our relationship with You.
We desire to know You more. We desire to set out on this path that You have set
before us of learning, and then faithfully practicing, Your spiritual disciplines.*

Notes and Prayer Requests

Use this space to write any key points, questions, or prayer requests from this week's study.

OBEDIENCE TO GOD'S COMMANDMENTS

IN THIS LESSON

Learning: What is the most important spiritual discipline?

Growing: How can I know what I'm supposed to do?

Obedience is not a popular idea today. People will be more readily accepted by the world at large if they are viewed as tolerant, compromising, lenient, or relational. The message from society today is that people must do their best to make everybody else happy and satisfied at all costs. However, God's Word calls believers in Christ to be obedient to all of God's laws, statutes, and commandments. Often, this requires going against the current thinking of the world. Yet there can be no spiritual growth—no genuine spiritual power or effective ministry to the lost—without obedience to God. A rebellious heart is contrary to spiritual strength.

Rebellion is the foremost reason for a lack of spiritual authority, a lack of intimacy with God, and a lack of genuine blessings and rewards from God. When most of us think of *rebels,* we think of juvenile delinquents, criminals, or those who are opposed to the establishment or current political order. However, the Bible defines *rebellion* in a much different way. It refers to *any* person as rebellious who enacts his or her own set of standards or does anything contrary to the commandments of God. Those who willfully choose their way over God's way are *rebels.*

1. "Do not imitate what is evil, but what is good. He who does good is of God, but he who does evil has not seen God" (3 John 1:11). In what ways have you struggled with rebellion in the past—not doing "what is good" or choosing your way over God's way?

2. "For rebellion is as the sin of witchcraft, and stubbornness is as iniquity and idolatry" (1 Samuel 15:23). Why does God say that a rebellious spirit is the same as the sin of witchcraft? In what ways is stubbornness the same as idolatry?

Our Relationship with God

As completely as the Lord stands against rebellion, He supports and upholds those who are obedient. In the Bible, we find that God honors those who are obedient to His commands. As the prophet Samuel stated, "Behold, to obey is better than sacrifice" (1 Samuel 15:22). At the heart of our relationship with God lies obedience to His commandments—an adherence to doing things *God's* way and a submission to seeking *God's* plan for our lives.

Even our salvation is an expression of obedience. We are not in a position to devise our own means of salvation or to choose the method, timetable, or circumstances for it. We must accept *God's* plan for our salvation and obey what He requires of us to receive His forgiveness of sins and eternal life. We must believe in Jesus Christ as the only complete sacrifice for our sin, receive the Holy Spirit into our lives, and willingly obey Him.

As the author of Hebrews said, "Though [Jesus] was a Son, yet He learned obedience by the things which He suffered. And having been perfected, He became the author of eternal salvation to all who obey Him" (Hebrews 5:8–9). None of us is in a position to require God to do things our way or to forgive us according to our plan. *All* of us are required by God to do things His way and to willingly submit ourselves to His plan for forgiveness and salvation.

When I was young, my grandfather once said to me, "Charles, if God tells you to run at a brick wall, then you run at that brick wall with all your strength, trusting Him to open the way for you." There simply is no substitute for obedience if you desire to see the full manifestation of God's trustworthiness, presence, and power in your life. Obedience is the key to you having a truly intimate relationship with God—and having such a relationship with your heavenly Father is what spiritual discipline is all about! The goal of all spiritual disciplines is knowing God more intimately and experiencing more of Him at work in you and through you.

3. "Has the LORD as great delight in burnt offerings and sacrifices, as in obeying the voice of the LORD? Behold, to obey is better than sacrifice" (1 Samuel 15:22). When have you tried to appease the Lord by sacrificing something while disobeying His Word in another area? What was the result?

....

....

....

....

....

....

....

....

....

....

4. In what area might the Lord be calling you to stricter obedience this week?

....

....

....

....

....

....

....

....

....

THE HINDRANCE OF SIN

Sin might be considered another word for acts of willful disobedience. It always carries negative consequences with it. Ultimately, a state of sinfulness brings about a person's spiritual death (see Romans 6:23). But even in the lives of those who have turned to God and received His forgiveness, sin is a tremendous hindrance to the work the Lord desires to do.

The writer of Hebrews said, "Therefore we also, since we are surrounded by so great a cloud of witnesses, let us lay aside every weight, and the sin which so easily ensnares us, and let us run with endurance the race that is set before us" (Hebrews 12:1). Sin is a weight and a snare. It slows us down, trips us up, and can delay or detour us from fulfilling God's purposes and plans. Part of our obedience to the Lord is to ask the Lord to forgive us *daily* for those things that we have thought, said, or done that are contrary to His commandments.

This is the only way we can avoid chastening from the Lord. It is the only way we can experience the fullness of God's blessings. It is the only way that we can cast off the hindrance of sin.

5. How can sin be like a runner carrying lead weights on his back? What is involved in "laying aside" those weights?

6. What "race" is set before you? What might be hindering you in that race at present?

....

....

....

....

....

....

....

....

....

....

A PASSION TO OBEY

There are several benchmarks by which we can evaluate if we are obeying God and developing spiritual discipline. *First, we need to consider if obedience is our bottom line.* Obedience to God must become the foundation of every decision we make. We must sift every decision through the will of God, asking, "Can I do this and be obedient to God and His commandments and plan for my life?" Even in those situations in which we feel inadequate and find ourselves struggling with fear, suffering, loss, or painful consequences, our desire must be to obey God's will.

Second, we must obey instantly. When the Holy Spirit speaks to our hearts, we shouldn't even stop to consider whether we will act. We just respond immediately.

Third, we have a yearning for the heart and mind of God. Our desire must be to learn more and more about how God works and what He wants for us . . . to have a yearning to seek the mind of God and know Him better. We certainly cannot learn *all* there is to know about God—we will never know Him with total intimacy—but our desire must be to know Him better and better. For us to grow spiritually, we must continually ask, "What is it that God truly desires for my life? How does God want me to act? What does He want me to say?" Our role is not to take our plans to God and ask Him to bless them. Our role is to ask God what He wants us to do with our lives—our time, our talents, and our material substance—and then do His bidding.

Fourth, we view God's opinion as all that matters. The opinions of others are never more important than the opinion of God. We must thus not concern ourselves about what others say—or even if they ridicule us—when it comes to following God's commands. The only acceptance that ultimately counts is God's acceptance. While we should seek out the counsel of godly people, we cannot fall into the trap of acting based on human consensus.

Fifth, we must be willing to accept the consequences of obedience. We have to be willing to accept the adverse consequences of our obedience. We are to suffer for Christ's sake—not *eager* to suffer, but joyful in the midst of suffering. As Jesus taught, "Blessed are those who are persecuted for righteousness' sake, for theirs is the kingdom of heaven" (Matthew 5:10).

7. "For none of us lives to himself, and no one dies to himself. For if we live, we live to the Lord; and if we die, we die to the Lord. Therefore, whether we live or die, we are the Lord's" (Romans 14:7–8). What does it mean to "live" or "die" to the Lord?

8. Consider your time, money, energy, and relationships. How well does your life reflect Paul's priorities as outlined in these verses?

....

....

....

....

....

....

....

....

....

THE REWARDS OF OBEDIENCE

There are a number of consequences of being obedient to God's Word . . and not all of them are positive. All who live in obedience to the Lord will suffer to a certain degree, because they are going against the grain of the world. However, the positive rewards from God far outweigh anything the world might do to us as obedient followers of Christ.

These rewards include a growing faith and blessings. We are able to see God's faithfulness in action and grow in our faith as a result. God then bestows His blessings on us, which may not only be spiritual blessings but also financial, material, and relational in nature.

God's rewards also include an enlarged view of Him. When we are obedient, we move into a more intimate relationship with God. The closer we come to God, the more we experience His love and the more we are able to see His omnipotence and omniscience (His infinite and absolute power and wisdom). We grow in reverence for God and have an increased sense of security in His deep and abiding love for us.

We gain a greater effectiveness in witnessing. Other people in our world—our family members, friends, coworkers, fellow church members, and even lost souls—will see our obedience and be affected by our steadfast faithfulness to God's commands. They can't help being influenced in a positive way toward the gospel, regardless of what they may claim.

Finally, we gain a greater ability to discern the Holy Spirit at work. We begin to hear the Holy Spirit with greater clarity and have greater recognition of His voice. We can discern with accuracy what the Holy Spirit directs us to and when and how to act.

Obedience is truly the bottom line for all spiritual discipline. It is the foundation for everything else we do. For example, we pray in obedience to God's command to pray. We read the Bible because we desire to know God's statutes and obey them, but also because we are commanded to study the Word. Our quest to know the Lord is rooted in obedience at all times.

Obedience is not the ultimate motivation for spiritual discipline. A love for God, a longing to know Him, and faith in Him are the true motives for the mature believer. Yet obedience is required if we are to grow spiritually and experience more of God's love.

9. "Whether it is pleasing or displeasing, we will obey the voice of the LORD our God to whom we send you, that it may be well with us when we obey the voice of the LORD our God" (Jeremiah 42:6). When have you obeyed the Lord's commands even though it seemed unpleasant? What was the result?

10. "For though we walk in the flesh, we do not war according to the flesh. For the weapons of our warfare are not carnal but mighty in God for pulling down strongholds" (2 Corinthians 10:3–4). In what war is the Christian engaged? What role does obedience to God's Word play in this warfare?

TODAY AND TOMORROW

Today: The Lord wants me to develop obedience above all other disciplines.

Tomorrow: This week I will ask the Lord to show me areas of my life where I need to obey Him more.

CLOSING PRAYER

. . . .

Lord, we acknowledge today that You desire for us to lead disciplined lives. Often it is so difficult for us to obey Your commands. Yet we know that we can only receive the life that You intend for us to have through complete obedience. Today, we pray that our life of obedience would serve as an example to the world. We desire for our testimony to be clear—and that our character, our conduct, and our conversation will all point others to you. We want our testimony to shout to the world that Jesus Christ is the Son of God, our only hope, and our source of genuine peace.

Notes and
Prayer Requests

Use this space to write any key points, questions, or prayer requests from this week's study.

CONFORMITY TO CHRIST

IN THIS LESSON

Learning: What does it mean to be conformed to Christ?

Growing: How is this done?

Psychologists and business leaders alike stress the positive benefits of setting good goals for ourselves. Having a goal in place triggers new behaviors, helps us sustain the momentum needed to persevere in reaching a new place in our lives, and helps us to identify and focus on our priorities. Setting goals helps us to establish what things are truly important to us—and then gives us a framework for how we can devote more of our time to those pursuits.

Goals come in various shapes and sizes. There are *long-term goals* that consist of plans that we make for our future. We achieve these types of goals as we proceed through life. We envision where we want to be (and what kind of person we want to be) in five years, ten years, or even twenty years down the road. Some examples of long-term goals could include going back to school for a Master's Degree, buying a house, running a marathon, or owning our own small business.

Short-term goals, on the other hand, consist of plans we want to achieve in the near future—typically in less than one year. Often, our short-term goals will serve as stepping-stones for reaching our long-term goals. Some examples include getting good grades in a current semester at school, learning how to fix an appliance, or preparing for an upcoming event.

It is important for us to consider both our short-term and long-term goals when it comes to setting *spiritual goals* for ourselves. We need long-term goals to get the "big picture" of where we want to be in the future and how that matches up with God's plans for our lives. We need short-term goals to envision the "step-by-step" process that we need to get us there. Without having good goals in place—and clear paths to reach them—we will rarely achieve all that we can achieve. This is true in the spiritual realm just as much as it is true in the worlds of business and personal finance, family life, education, or physical fitness.

I believe the apostle Paul clearly stated in Romans what the spiritual goal should be for every believer in Christ. As he wrote, "We know that all things work together for good to those who love God, to those who are the called according to His purpose. For whom He foreknew, He also predestined to be conformed to the image of His Son, that He might be the firstborn among many brethren. Moreover whom He predestined, these He also called; whom He called, these He also justified; and whom He justified, these He also glorified" (Romans 8:28–30).

1. What things does God work together to produce good in a Christian's life?

2. If God works all things together for good, what does that mean regarding the present circumstances in your life? Regarding the future? Regarding the past?

THE CONFORMITY PROCESS

I want to call your attention to three key truths found in this passage from the apostle Paul. I believe these truths will be important for you as you practice basic spiritual disciplines and seek to grow in Christ. They will help you understand the type of person God wants you to be as you seek to set good goals that will yield greater spiritual maturity in your life.

First, you are destined to be conformed to Christ. From the beginning of time, God chose you to be His beloved child and be conformed to the image of Christ. As Paul said, "For whom [God] foreknew, He also pre-destined to be conformed to the image of His Son" (Romans 8:29). This phrase, "to be conformed" implies that at present, you are *not* conformed to Christ's image. We certainly know this is true for each and every one of us. None of us has lived a sinless life or is without fault. "All have sinned and fall short of the glory of God" (3:23).

We all come from imperfect backgrounds. We all have experiences that have left us wounded and scarred. All of us require healing in some area. No matter how spiritually mature we are, there is always *more* that must be changed in us for us to be *fully* like Christ Jesus. Only God can say, "I change not," because only God can say, "I do not need change." We can all look in the mirror and say, "Lord, change me in the ways that I need to be changed."

Second, you are conformed to Christ's image. This means that you are an accurate and total reflection of Christ. In other words, when others look at you, they do not see anything in what you say or do that is *con-trary* to what Jesus would have said and done if He were on earth in fleshly form today. A person who is *completely* conformed to Christ's image thinks, speaks, and acts exactly as Christ would think, speak, and act in any situation.

Again, we know this is not true for any person! We *all* have sinned and continue to sin, even though we have no desire to sin. Even the apostle Paul lamented about this reality in his life: "For what I am do-ing, I do not understand. For what I will to do, that I do not practice; but what I hate, that I do. . . . O wretched man that I am! Who will deliver me from this body of death?" (7:15, 24). We are imperfect, fi-nite, fleshly creatures. Nevertheless, God calls us to grow in godliness until that day He perfects us and we put on the full image of Christ.

Third, this is God's work . . . not your own. Paul never said we are to strive to be perfect. He said this would be the work of the Holy Spirit in us. "Moreover whom *He* predestined, these *He* also called;

whom *He* called, these *He* also justified; and whom *He* justified, these *He* also glorified" (8:30, emphasis added). It is *God* who does the predestining, calling, justifying, and the glorifying. The conforming work in us is not something for which we are totally responsible. We are to live by faith, obey, and then trust God to do the transforming work in us.

3. "But we all, with unveiled face, beholding as in a mirror the glory of the Lord, are being transformed into the same image from glory to glory, just as by the Spirit of the Lord" (2 Corinthians 3:18). How does God transform you to become more like Christ? What is God's role in this process? What is your role?

4. "Do not lie to one another, since you have put off the old man with his deeds, and have put on the new man who is renewed in knowledge according to the image of Him who created him" (Colossians 3:9–10). Who is the "old man" and "new man"?

5. What is involved in "putting off" the old man and "putting on" the new man?

....

....

....

....

....

....

....

....

DEVELOPING THE MIND OF CHRIST

As believers in Christ, we should never have any doubts about what we are to do in this life. We are never to be confused about what long-term or short-term goals we should set when it comes to our spiritual growth or what pursuits we should follow. Our ultimate goal in life is to do those things that conform us to Christ's image. As Paul wrote, "I have been crucified with Christ; it is no longer I who live, but Christ lives in me" (Galatians 2:20). Our past lives—where we sinfully pursued our own interests—have been put to death. Now we pursue Christ. We seek to develop His mindset so we can increasingly be transformed into His likeness.

So, how do we do this? How do we develop the mind of Christ? Most of us have seen the bracelets and bumper stickers that say "WWJD," meaning "What Would Jesus Do?" While that is a wonderful message, it is far from complete. We are not only to *do* what Jesus would *do* but also to *say* what He would say, *think* what He thinks, and *believe* what He believes. As Paul taught, "Do not be conformed to this world, but be transformed by the renewing of your mind, that you may prove what is that good and acceptable and perfect will of God" (Romans 12:2).

From this verse, we see four truths on what it means to have the mind of Christ. *First, we have a desire to serve others.* When we think as Jesus thinks, we have an impulse to help others in need. We do not even stop to think about whether we *should* help that person who is in trouble. We move immediately to that person's side to offer whatever assistance we can give, whether that is practical or spiritual.

Second, we have an understanding of right and wrong. When we think as Jesus thinks, we have righteous and pure thoughts. We know God's absolutes and God's desires for good. We do not even need to contemplate whether an activity or thought is *right*—we know immediately whether something lines up with God's commandments and His nature. We have the ability to discern a lie from the truth and to know whether a thought is a temptation from the enemy or a directive from the Holy Spirit.

Third, we are able to discern spiritual matters. When we think as Jesus thinks, we are rooted in obedience to God's commandments. We know God's nature, so we can discern between false and true doctrines. We are able to judge the biblical authenticity of spiritual manifestations. John wrote, "Beloved, do not believe every spirit, but test the spirits, whether they are of God" (1 John 4:1). When we have the mind of Christ, we know how to "test the spirits" and determine if something is truly from the Lord.

Fourth, we make wise decisions and choices. When we think as Jesus thinks, we know how to make godly decisions, including how to choose our friends. Of course, none of us will instantly have the mind of Christ on our conversion. Just as newborn babies grow in their ability to understand the world, so newborn Christians must grow in their understanding of God's nature, God's commandments, and the fullness of His Word.

Furthermore, our will is always involved. We must *want* to develop the mind of Christ. We must *seek* to know God's Word so that we can find God's answers, direction, and solutions. We must *ask* God to impart His wisdom to us each and every day.

6. "Do not be conformed to this world" (Romans 12:2). What does it mean to be "conformed to this world"? Give specific examples.

....

....

....

....

....

....

7. "Be transformed by the renewing of your mind" (Romans 12:2). What does it mean to renew your mind? How is this done?

....

....

....

....

....

....

....

8. In what areas would you like to see growth in developing more of the mindset of Christ?

....

....

....

....

....

....

CONFORMITY THROUGH SUFFERING

There is another aspect to our being conformed to Christ that many of us do not like to consider: *suffering.* The Christian life is not immune to pain. In fact, in many ways, the call of Christ *is* a call to suffer. It is a call to identify with those who are hurting, which always requires a sacrifice of self and laying aside our pride. The call of Christ is also a call to be willing to experience the persecution of the world and to suffer rejection. We *identify* with Christ in our sufferings, for He, too, suffered and aligned Himself with those who suffered.

The most fertile time of spiritual growth for many Christians comes during a period of suffering—a crisis, illness, persecution, loss, pain, or rejection. Suffering is the means God often uses to perfect us and to craft us into the true character of Christ. As James wrote, for this reason we can actually rejoice in our sufferings: "My brethren, count it all joy when you fall into various trials, knowing that the testing of your faith produces patience. But let patience have its perfect work, that you may be perfect and complete, lacking nothing" (James 1:2-4).

Today, I challenge you not to shy away from difficulties or troublesome people. Rather, I encourage you to see them as opportunities to minister the love of Christ!

9. "Since Christ suffered for us in the flesh, arm yourselves also with the same mind, for he who has suffered in the flesh has ceased from sin, that he no longer should live the rest of his time in the flesh for the lusts of men, but for the will of God" (1 Peter 4:1-2). How do you arm yourself with the mind of Christ?

10. As you look back, what are some of the spiritual benefits you have received after going through a time of crisis or suffering?

TODAY AND TOMORROW

Today: God wants me to become more
and more like His Son.

Tomorrow: I will ask the Lord this week to
show me ways that I can imitate Him.

CLOSING PRAYER

Heavenly Father, we want to develop the mindset and character of Christ. We ask the Holy Spirit to come into our lives to enable us to think the way that Jesus thinks. We desire for the Holy Spirit to lead us to act as Jesus acts—and to speak to others as the Lord would speak to them. We love You and thank You for Your forgiveness and for cleansing our hearts. Please sink these truths deep within our souls. We choose to put You and Your Word first in all things.

NOTES AND
PRAYER REQUESTS

· ·

Use this space to write any key points, questions, or prayer requests from this week's study.

A Personal Study of the Scriptures

IN THIS LESSON

Learning: Where does the Bible come
into this process?

Growing: How can I hope to understand
what the Bible teaches?

As believers in Christ, we must know God's Word if we desire to develop the mind of Christ, move into obedience to God's commandments, and become more conformed to Christ. If we want to experience more of the presence and power of God, we must be disciplined to read and study God's Word for ourselves. There is no substitute for it!

Our study of God's Word must first be personal. Many people take a Bible to church each Sunday but let it gather dust the rest of the week. Some say, "I listen to sermons about the Bible." Others tell me they read books about what God says in the Bible. None of these are a substitute for studying God's Word, because *knowing* the Bible is more than just knowing its content. It is knowing how to *apply* God's Word to our daily lives.

We each are at different levels of spiritual maturity. So we *must* read and study the Bible for ourselves to allow it to speak to our unique circumstances. The primary way God speaks to us is through His Word. Certainly, He speaks through other means, but His *primary* way of speaking today is through His Word. As you read His Word, ask the Holy Spirit to give you understanding and impart to you the specific knowledge that you need directly from God.

Our study of God's Word must also be daily. For us to continually grow in the Lord and remain strong in Him, we must read God's Word daily, simply because our lives are lived daily. A part of the Lord's Prayer is, "Give us this day our daily bread" (Matthew 6:11). *Bread* refers not only to physical bread, but also to the spiritual bread we need to feed our souls. No person eats only once a week. We all eat daily . . . usually several times a day. What is true for the physical is also true for the spiritual. We need to read the Bible daily to give our minds and hearts the spiritual nutrition they need to face life's daily demands.

The more we read the Bible—asking God to reveal Christ to us through the Holy Spirit—the greater our understanding will be of God's commandments and goals for your life. We will see more clearly how the Lord wants us to live. We will discover specific guidance for the decisions we are currently facing. We will understand how to apply what we read to our life. Specifically, we will develop a more godly life, understand our eternal purpose, comprehend our role in God's plan, discover how to have victory over Satan, and receive specific direction.

LEAD A GODLY LIFE

Each of us is called to live a godly life—one that is holy, pure, and righteous. Again and again, we find stories in the Bible that might be described as "before and after" spiritual makeovers. Again and again, we find God's commands to put off our old nature and put on the character of Christ Jesus. The more we read our Bibles, the more we are going to come face-to-face with practical changes that God wants us to make in the way that we think, speak, and act.

Consider this applicable passage from Ephesians: "Therefore, putting away lying, 'Let each one of you speak truth with his neighbor,' for we are members of one another. 'Be angry, and do not sin': do not let the sun go down on your wrath, nor give place to the devil. Let him who stole steal no longer, but rather let him labor, working with his hands what is good, that he may have something to give him who has need. Let no corrupt word proceed out of your mouth, but what is good for necessary edification, that it may impart grace to the hearers. . . . Let all bitterness, wrath, anger, clamor, and evil speaking be put away from you, with all malice. And be kind to one another, tenderhearted, forgiving one another, even as God in Christ forgave you" (Ephesians 4:25–29, 31–32).

In just a few verses, the apostle Paul provides us with several specific instructions about what it means to live a godly life. There can be little room for misinterpretation of these verses! God's Word continually challenges us to live sinless lives. He wants us to live genuinely good, righteous lives. He makes it possible for us to live such lives by the power of His Holy Spirit.

1. How would you define bitterness, wrath, and clamor versus being tenderhearted and forgiving? Give some practical examples.

2. "Whom will he teach knowledge? And whom will he make to understand the message? Those just weaned from milk? Those just drawn from the breasts? For precept must be upon precept, precept upon precept, line upon line, line upon line, here a little, there a little" (Isaiah 28:9–10). What does Isaiah mean when he speaks about learning from "precept upon precept"? How does this apply to daily Bible reading?

....

....

....

....

....

....

....

....

....

REMEMBER YOUR ETERNAL PURPOSE

Each of us is called to invest our life in those things that have eternal purpose. From cover to cover, the Bible speaks of God's everlasting nature, His desire for us to be with Him for all eternity, and His eternal purposes. The more you read your Bible, the more you will gain an eternal perspective and grow in your understanding that only those things that are linked to Christ Jesus truly last.

You will also gain an understanding that there is no such thing as a "secular job." All jobs exist so that Christ might be manifested through them. God's love, healing, and forgiveness can be made known through all situations. No part of your life is apart from Christ. He desires to touch every aspect of your life with His eternal presence and power. Because of this, your life has tremendous meaning. The greatest satisfaction in life comes in knowing that Christ is in you and is accomplishing His eternal purposes not only in you but through you.

3. "Do not be unwise, but understand what the will of the Lord is" (Ephesians 5:17). How does a person "understand what the will of the Lord is"? What is required of you? What is God's role?

....

....

....

....

....

....

....

....

....

4. What part does the Bible play in that process?

....

....

....

....

....

....

....

....

CONSIDER YOUR ROLE IN GOD'S PLAN

Each of us is called to a specific role as part of God's greater purpose. The more you read your Bible, the more you will gain a vision for those greater purposes and plans of God. You will see yourself in the context of God's greater will. No longer will the big "I" be at the center of the universe—rather, Christ will be central in your life.

As you read God's Word, you will gain an understanding that God does not exist for *you*, but rather, you exist for *God*. God doesn't exist to be molded into your purpose. Rather, you were created to be part of His purpose. God's purpose is for you to bring glory to Christ Jesus and that, by your witness, the world may come to know Jesus Christ as Savior and Lord.

Jesus challenged His disciples, "Go therefore and make disciples of all the nations, baptizing them in the name of the Father and of the Son and of the Holy Spirit, teaching them to observe all things that I have commanded you; and lo, I am with you always, even to the end of the age" (Matthew 28:19–20). To make disciples, you must be prepared and willing to teach others everything you learn from God's Word. This teaching does not have to be formal. You can teach the truth of God in your daily conversations and by being a witness for Christ every time you have an opportunity to share the gospel.

5. "Go therefore and make disciples of all the nations" (Matthew 28:19). How can an untrained Christian "make disciples of all the nations"? In what ways can you be teaching others about God's Word?

6. "[Teach] them to observe all things that I have commanded you" (Matthew 28:20). What things has Jesus commanded you? How well are you obeying those commands?

....

....

....

....

....

....

....

....

RECOGNIZE YOU HAVE VICTORY IN CHRIST

Each of us is called to have victory over the enemy of our souls. The more we read the Bible, the more we learn how to realize this victory over sin and over the enemy of our souls. We have greater strength to withstand the devil's temptations.

In the Gospels, we discover that when Jesus was tempted by the devil, He did not respond with human wisdom. Rather, he fought against Satan by quoting the Word of God. Read the account of Jesus' temptations and note how He replied to each one:

Then Jesus was led up by the Spirit into the wilderness to be tempted by the devil. And when He had fasted forty days and forty nights, afterward He was hungry. Now when the tempter came to Him, he said, "If You are the Son of God, command that these stones become bread."

But He answered and said, "It is written, 'Man shall not live by bread alone, but by every word that proceeds from the mouth of God.'"

> Then the devil took Him up into the holy city, set Him on the pinnacle of the temple, and said to Him, "If You are the Son of God, throw Yourself down." . . .
>
> Jesus said to him, "It is written again, 'You shall not tempt the Lord your God.'"
>
> Again, the devil took Him up on an exceedingly high mountain, and showed Him all the kingdoms of the world and their glory. And he said to Him, "All these things I will give You if You will fall down and worship me."
>
> Then Jesus said to him, "Away with you, Satan! For it is written, 'You shall worship the Lord your God, and Him only you shall serve'" [Deuteronomy 6:13] (Matthew 4:1–10).

Notice in this passage how many times Jesus quoted from Scripture—each from the Old Testament book of Deuteronomy: "Man shall not live by bread alone; but man lives by every word that proceeds from the mouth of the Lord" (8:3); "You shall not tempt the Lord your God" (6:16); "You shall fear the Lord your God and serve Him, and shall take oaths in His name" (6:13). To be able to say to the devil, "It is written," you must first know *what* is written!

7. "Your word I have hidden in my heart, that I might not sin against You" (Psalm 119:11). What does it mean to hide God's Word in your heart? How is this done?

8. "Then the devil left Him, and behold, angels came and ministered to Him" (Matthew 4:11). How did Jesus' knowledge of Scripture help Him face temptation? When has knowledge of God's Word helped you in the past?

....

....

....

....

....

....

....

....

LOOK FOR GOD'S DIRECTION

How do daily Bible reading and Bible study differ? Bible *study* is an intense search of God's Word to learn more about what God has to say on a particular subject. Quite often, Bible study is aimed at finding specific answers to specific needs, concerns, questions, or problems.

For example, you may have questions about why God acts in particular ways. You may question why God fails to act in a particular situation in the way you think He should. You have questions about what God wants you to do, which decision you should make, or which path you should follow. These questions should motivate you to go to your Bible to study what God says on the matter. An honest question is always an excellent beginning point for Bible study!

The apostle Paul wrote to Timothy: "Be diligent to present yourself approved to God, a worker who does not need to be ashamed, rightly dividing the word of truth" (2 Timothy 2:15). To "rightly divide" the word of truth means to see the *whole* of God's truth and separate out anything that might be a lie. It is a sifting process . . . taking out anything that might pollute or detract from the truth. Bible study will help you to refine your understanding of God's Word.

In the refinement of metals such as silver and gold, the metal is heated to an extremely high temperature and brought to a liquid state. The lighter impurities in the metal float to the top of the liquid and are skimmed off. The heavier and more valuable metal remains at the bottom. That is what happens when you engage in a diligent study of God's Word on a particular matter. You come to an understanding that is clearer, purer, and more concentrated. You truly *know* what God has to say on a matter!

9. "Be diligent to present yourself approved to God, a worker who does not need to be ashamed, rightly dividing the word of truth" (2 Timothy 2:15). What does it mean to be "rightly dividing the word of truth"? How is this done? What is your role?

10. Why does Paul command you to "be diligent" in this matter? Why is this necessary?

TODAY AND TOMORROW

Today: God reveals Himself clearly to His people through His Word.

Tomorrow: I will begin a daily habit of reading the Bible this week.

CLOSING PRAYER

Lord, we love You and praise You for giving us this precious book that we call the sacred Scriptures. The Word of God. The Holy Bible. We pray that You will make the truth of Your Word real to every believer and non-believer alike. Bring about conviction and correction in any area where we have gone astray from Your Word. Help us today to study Your Word every day so that we can learn how to truly apply it to our lives. We thank You for Your faithfulness to us.

NOTES AND
PRAYER REQUESTS

· ·

Use this space to write any key points, questions, or prayer requests
from this week's study.

GETTING TO KNOW THE LORD

IN THIS LESSON

Learning: What is the purpose of prayer?

Growing: How am I supposed to pray—
for myself and others?

There is only one way to develop a deep friendship . . . and that is to spend time with a person. We share our mutual experiences and communicate our ideas, dreams, hopes, and beliefs to that individual. Spending time together, sharing experiences, talking things over—these basic ingredients for developing a relationship with another human being are the same basic ingredients for developing a relationship with God.

Are you aware that we are commanded to pray? Jesus said to His disciples, "Watch and pray, lest you enter into temptation. The spirit indeed is willing, but the flesh is weak" (Matthew 26:41). Prayer is not just a good idea. It is God's command. It is a requirement if we are to become and remain strong in the Lord and develop an intimate relationship with Him. Keeping this in mind, in this lesson we will look at seven aspects of prayer that we should consider as we seek to become spiritually disciplined and to grow spiritually.

1. What are some ways that you develop your friendships with others? What are some practices you employ to develop your friendship with God?

2. "Let us therefore come boldly to the throne of grace, that we may obtain mercy and find grace to help in time of need" (Hebrews 4:16). How are you to approach God in prayer?

PRAY CONTINUALLY AND PETITION GOD FOR YOUR NEEDS

First, we are called to pray continually. Many Christians pray only in church. Some say grace at mealtimes. Others say bedtime prayers with their children. All of these are appropriate times to pray, but the command to Christians from God's Word is to "pray without ceasing" (1 Thessalonians 5:17). We pray at all times, without ceasing, by living in an attitude of prayer.

To *pray* is simply to communicate with God. This includes both talking *and* listening to God. To pray without ceasing is to talk to God about virtually everything and to feel free to do so at any time and in any place. It is to discuss with God any problem or need that we face. It is to praise or thank God immediately when good things come our way. It is to converse with Him about decisions we must make, circumstances that require our involvement, and issues we must resolve. It is to be constantly on the alert to see what God wants us to see and to have spiritual ears open to hear what God wants us to hear.

Over the centuries, God's people developed a habit of praying at morning, noon, and night. Prayer was not limited to these times but was offered as a community at these times every day. I know of no better way to start a day and end a day than in prayer! The greatest way to frame a day is to frame it in prayer—seeking God's guidance, protection, and wisdom for the coming day as you pray in the morning and thanking God for His abundant provision to you as you prepare to sleep in the evening.

I believe God is pleased when we set aside specific times to pray. To do so is to make prayer an intentional part of our lives. It is to develop a *habit* of prayer, which is one of the most beneficial habits we could ever develop. It is to say to God, to ourselves, and to others, "I value my relationship with God, and I am setting aside a part of every day just to be with Him and to talk things over with Him."

Second, we are to petition God for our needs. As we engage in this practice of ongoing prayer, we are to ask God to meet our needs—including our need for forgiveness. Remember, it is not self-centered for us to pray for ourselves, our family, or our loved ones. God wants us to pray for our needs! The nature of the need may be physical, financial, emotional, or spiritual—no need is too small or too great to take to God. A part of our prayer every day should also be a prayer confessing our sins and asking God to forgive us, cleanse us, and help us make the necessary changes in our lives so that we do not keep repeating sin.

3. "Confess your trespasses to one another, and pray for one another, that you may be healed. The effective, fervent prayer of a righteous man avails much" (James 5:16). Why are we commanded to confess our sins to one another?

4. What is "fervent prayer"? How is it different from other forms of prayer?

PRAISE GOD AND HAVE AN ATTITUDE OF FORGIVENESS

Third, we are to accompany our petitions with praise and thanksgiving. Paul urged the early church to pray without ceasing: "Rejoice always, pray without ceasing, in everything give thanks; for this is the will of God in Christ Jesus for you" (1 Thessalonians 5:16–18).

We rejoice, give praise, and express our gratitude for having a relationship with the Lord. We praise Him for His wonderful deeds, for all that He is, and for all that He has done, including the things He has done and will do in our lives. We then make our petitions. We tell God our concerns and needs. Finally, we give thanks that He is already working on our behalf to cause *all* things to be used for our eternal good (see Romans 8:28). Our prayers take on a much different tone and character when we begin them with praise and end them with thanksgiving!

When Jesus gave His model prayer to His disciples, He began it with words of praise: "Our Father in heaven, hallowed be Your name" (Matthew 6:9). To *hallow* the Lord's name is to declare it holy and worthy to be lifted higher than any other name. When we say, "Hallowed be Your name," we are praising the name of the Lord, exalting Him to a position of absolute supremacy. Look also at how the Lord ended His model prayer: "For Yours is the kingdom and the power and the glory forever" (6:13). He ended with praise and thanksgiving. The overall model of the Lord's Prayer is praise, petition, praise.

Fourth, we adopt an attitude of forgiveness. We are to pray with an attitude of forgiveness toward others. The Bible makes it clear that unless we forgive others, we cannot receive God's forgiveness. Our unforgiving attitude acts as a barrier, keeping us from receiving the fullness of what God desires to give us. As Jesus taught, "If you forgive men their trespasses, your heavenly Father will also forgive you. But if you do not forgive men their trespasses, neither will your Father forgive your trespasses" (6:14–15).

5. "Be anxious for nothing, but in everything by prayer and supplication, with thanksgiving, let your requests be made known to God" (Philippians 4:6). Why does Paul command you not to be anxious? How does anxiety hinder prayer?

....

....

....

....

....

....

....

....

6. "If you do not forgive men their trespasses, neither will your Father forgive your trespasses" (Matthew 6:15). Is there anyone in your life that you have not forgiven? How might this be preventing God's forgiveness in your own life?

....

....

....

....

....

....

....

....

PRAY TO THE LORD WITHOUT DOUBT

Fifth, we are to pray without doubting and without losing heart. James said in one of his teachings that we are to ask God for wisdom: "Let him ask in faith, with no doubting, for he who doubts is like a wave of the sea driven and tossed by the wind. For let not that man suppose that he will receive anything from the Lord; he is a double-minded man, unstable in all his ways" (James 1:6–8). This is true in our prayers for wisdom—and in *all* our prayers.

Jesus taught this lesson to His disciples by causing a fig tree to become withered. "Now in the morning, as He returned to the city, He was hungry. And seeing a fig tree by the road, He came to it and found nothing on it but leaves, and said to it, 'Let no fruit grow on you ever again.' Immediately the fig tree withered away" (Matthew 21:18–19). When the disciples saw this, they marveled, saying, "How did the fig tree wither away so soon?" (verse 20).

Jesus responded, "Assuredly, I say to you, if you have faith and do not doubt, you will not only do what was done to the fig tree, but also if you say to this mountain, 'Be removed and be cast into the sea,' it will be done. And whatever things you ask in prayer, believing, you will receive" (verses 21–22). To pray without doubt and without losing heart is to pray with *faith*. At all times, our prayers must be steeped in faith if they are to be effective.

7. "He who doubts is like a wave of the sea driven and tossed by the wind" (James 1:6). How is a person who lacks faith like a wave tossed by the wind?

8. "Whatever things you ask in prayer, believing, you will receive" (Matthew 21:22). What promise are you given when you ask God in faith and according to His will?

....

....

....

....

....

....

....

....

....

....

PRAY FOR YOUR LEADERS AND INTERCEDE FOR OTHERS

Sixth, we are to pray for those in authority over us. Christians around the world are able to prosper spiritually under all kinds of governments, especially those that allow religious freedoms. We are able to work in any kind of environment and prosper, especially if the "boss" allows expressions of faith and opportunities for time off to worship with other believers.

Our prayer should be that our leaders make decisions that allow us to live in peace and share the gospel. We should pray that as believers in Christ, we will be allowed to live in an environment that is conducive to godliness and reverence. The apostle Paul taught, "Therefore I exhort first of all that supplications, prayers, intercessions, and giving of thanks be made for all men, for kings and all who are in authority, that we may lead a quiet and peaceable life in all godliness and reverence. For this is good and acceptable in the sight of God our Savior, who desires all men to be saved and to come to the knowledge of the truth" (1 Timothy 2:1-2).

Seventh, we are to intercede in prayer for others. We are to ask for the prayers of others and offer prayers for those in need. God desires for us to be in a giving and receiving relationship with others and that, as the body of Christ, we bear one another's burdens. As Paul wrote, "Bear one another's burdens, and so fulfill the law of Christ" (Galatians 6:2).

The disciples of Jesus were quick to ask for prayer and to offer prayer for others in need. In the book of Acts, we read how Peter and John were detained by the Jewish authorities for healing a man in the name of Jesus. Later, they were released but warned to never again speak in His name. The disciples went to their companions and reported what had happened.

The group responded with this prayer: "Lord, look on their threats, and grant to Your servants that with all boldness they may speak Your word, by stretching out Your hand to heal, and that signs and wonders may be done through the name of Your holy Servant Jesus" (Acts 4: 29–30). If Peter and John needed the prayers of others, how much more so do each of us need the prayers of fellow believers in Christ Jesus?

If you ever question what to pray for another Christian, let me suggest Paul's prayer for the Colossians: "[We] do not cease to pray for you, and to ask that you may be filled with the knowledge of His will in all wisdom and spiritual understanding; that you may walk worthy of the Lord, fully pleasing Him, being fruitful in every good work and increasing in the knowledge of God; strengthened with all might, according to His glorious power, for all patience and longsuffering with joy; giving thanks to the Father who has qualified us to be partakers of the inheritance of the saints in the light" (Colossians 1:9–12). This prayer covers many of the basics that we know with certainty are the will of God.

If we pray regularly with faith, perseverance, praise, and thanksgiving, we can expect answers from God! We can expect God to move obstacles, change situations, and bring forth blessings. We can expect to experience a deepening intimacy in our relationship with the Lord. We can expect to grow spiritually and to be strong in faith. God hears our prayers. He answers them for our eternal benefit. And He invites us to an ever-deepening relationship with Him.

9. "Let every soul be subject to the governing authorities. For there is no authority except from God, and the authorities that exist are appointed by God" (Romans 13:1). Why does Paul say we should submit to authority? How does this relate to praying for those who are in positions of authority over you?

10. "I desire therefore that the men pray everywhere, lifting up holy hands, without wrath and doubting" (1 Timothy 2:8). What does it mean to lift up holy hands? How can wrath hinder our prayers? How might wrath and doubting be related?

TODAY AND TOMORROW

Today: Prayer for myself and others is a vital
part of growing in Christ.

Tomorrow: I will add prayer to my daily schedule
of Bible reading this week.

CLOSING PRAYER

Father, You are a sovereign, holy, righteous, perfect, and all-loving Father who desires to get to know each of us personally and individually. This is so wonderful that it is beyond our comprehension! We love You, thank You, and praise You for loving us so much. Today, we pray that we will never miss an opportunity to spend time in Your presence. Let us be willing to not only speak but also to listen—open to anything You want to reveal in our hearts.

NOTES AND
PRAYER REQUESTS

Use this space to write any key points, questions, or prayer requests from this week's study.

LOOKING FOR CHRIST IN ALL THINGS

IN THIS LESSON

Learning: Does God speak to us in ways besides the Bible?

Growing: How can I learn to hear His voice?

In the last chapter, we touched on the fact that listening is a crucial part of all communication, including our interaction with God. Listening involves far more than simply waiting for God to reply to our prayers. It involves an *active listening*—an intent watching and waiting—for God to speak to us continually. Listening is to always be our attitude toward the Lord. We are to expect God to speak to us and to keep our hearts and minds open to Him so He might speak by any means at any time. To listen in this way is to be available to the Lord without hindrance.

There is a great story told in the Bible about the importance of making listening to God a priority in our lives. One day, Jesus and His disciples travelled to the home of Mary, Martha, and Lazarus in the village of Bethany. As we read, "Martha welcomed Him into her house. And she had a sister called Mary, who also sat at Jesus' feet and heard His word. But Martha was distracted with much serving" (Luke 10:38–40). Mary was sitting at Jesus' feet. She was listening. She was learning. She longed to know the things that Jesus knew.

What Mary did was not considered proper for a woman in those days. The proper place for a woman in those days was in the kitchen. But Mary's love for Jesus was greater than any concerns about social norms. She was going to take advantage of sitting at His feet, listening to Him, learning from Him, and longing to have the same qualities in her life as Him.

Meanwhile, Martha *was* the kitchen. She was running in circles, twisted in all different ways, trying to get everything done. She felt overwhelmed by many tasks . . . and she was clearly annoyed with her sister. She says to Jesus, "Lord, do You not care that my sister has left me to serve alone? Therefore tell her to help me" (verse 40). I like how Jesus responds: "Martha, Martha, you are worried and troubled about many things. But one thing is needed, and Mary has chosen that good part, which will not be taken away from her" (verses 41–42).

Jesus tells Martha that He recognizes she is troubled about a lot of things. In fact, she is troubled about *too* many things. She is on an uneven keel. He reminds Martha that her sister has chosen the most important thing—and He is not going to take that away from her. Mary is *listening* to Jesus. She has chosen the right priority: spending time with Christ.

1. "But seek first the kingdom of God and His righteousness, and all these things shall be added to you. Therefore do not worry about tomorrow, for tomorrow will worry about its own things. Sufficient for the day is its own trouble" (Matthew 6:33–34).

What does Jesus say in this passage as it relates to your priorities in life?

....

....

....

....

....

....

....

....

2. What promise is provided in this passage for those who seek God's kingdom first? How does this relate to spending time in prayer listening for God's voice?

....

....

....

....

....

....

....

....

WAIT IN GOD'S PRESENCE

Like Mary, we need to make listening to Christ a priority. This involves our attitudes, which are mental and emotional habits. Like all habits, we can practice them and develop them over time. We can *choose* what we will think about and how we will respond to life. The more we make positive, godly choices in our thought life, the more likely those choices are going to be our *habitual responses* in times of crisis or deep need. I believe there are four key ways that you can discipline yourself to develop this habit of listening and being available to the Lord.

First, wait in God's presence. It is easy to just spend your prayer time talking to the Lord without spending any time waiting in silence to see how He might respond. So take time to just sit or kneel in silence before the Lord. Empty your mind of all other thoughts. Concentrate on His Word and His presence with you. Ask Him to speak to you.

Many people today seem to be uncomfortable with silence, especially if they are alone. However, it is in the silence that you will be able to hear the voice of the Lord. The prophet Elijah came to understand this. After receiving a death threat from Queen Jezebel, he escaped to an isolated desert area. There, in a cave, he heard the Lord tell him to go outside. Elijah obeyed, and "a great and strong wind tore into the mountains and broke the rocks in pieces before the LORD, but the LORD was not in the wind; and after the wind an earthquake, but the LORD was not in the earthquake; and after the earthquake a fire, but the LORD was not in the fire; and after the fire a still small voice" (1 Kings 19:11–13). God spoke in a "still, small voice."

3. What was God teaching Elijah by contrasting the mighty wind, earthquake, and fire with the still, small voice? What does this teach concerning prayer?

....

....

....

....

....

....

....

....

....

4. "But those who wait on the LORD shall renew their strength; they shall mount up with wings like eagles, they shall run and not be weary, they shall walk and not faint" (Isaiah 40:31). What are some of the benefits of waiting in God's presence?

....

....

....

....

....

....

....

....

....

....

PRACTICE FREQUENT PRAISE

Second, praise the Lord often, regardless of your circumstances. Many people only praise God when something good happens or when they receive an unexpected blessing. But the Lord is worthy of our praise at *all* times and in *all* circumstances. Do not praise the Lord on the basis of circumstances but on the basis of *who He is* in the midst of those circumstances. Do not praise the Lord because of the way you *feel* but because of *who He is* and the way He feels about you!

In addition, don't limit your praise to the song service at church. Praise the Lord often, in both words and songs that you create spontaneously. All around you, at all times, you can find countless things for which to praise the Lord. Look for those things and voice your praise and thanksgiving to God. When you are alone in your car, in an elevator, in your office, or in your home, take the opportunity to voice praise to God for who He is, what He has done in the past, what He is doing in your life and in the lives of your loved ones, and what He will do for you throughout all eternity. You can never run out of things for which to praise God!

When you voice praise to the Lord, you will experience the presence of God with you. The Bible tells us the Lord is enthroned in the praises of His people (see Psalm 22:3). The greater your praise, the smaller your problems will appear. The more frequent your praise, the less you will find yourself with time to worry or feel anxious. The more you praise the Lord, the more you are going to see things that are worthy of His praise. Your entire attitude will shift from being you-centered and problem-centered to being God-centered and answer-centered.

5. "Praise God in His sanctuary; praise Him in His mighty firmament! Praise Him for His mighty acts; praise Him according to His excellent greatness! Praise Him with the sound of the trumpet; praise Him with the lute and harp! Praise Him with the timbrel and dance; praise Him with stringed instruments and flutes! Praise Him with loud cymbals; praise Him with clashing cymbals!" (Psalm 150:1–5). What does this psalm suggest about when, where, and the ways in which you can praise the Lord?

6. "You are my God. I will exalt You, I will praise Your name, for You have done wonderful things; Your counsels of old are faithfulness and truth" (Isaiah 25:1). What are some ways you can praise God right now for all that He has done on your behalf?

SEE CHRIST IN ALL THINGS

Third, look for evidence of Christ in every circumstance. The Lord is present in even the worst disaster or most overwhelming crisis. When you find yourself confused, frustrated, or overwhelmed by the situations around you, the best question we can ask is, "Father, what do You want to do in this situation?" Asking that question immediately shifts your focus off the problem and onto the One who has all the answers and provision in His hand.

The Lord is utterly faithful, and He is with you *always*. There is no moment of any day of your life that He is beyond hearing your heart's cry or your sincere question. Remember that how and when He chooses to speak to you is up to Him. You cannot force the Lord to answer you *when* you desire an answer or *in the way* you desire. The person who asks a question of the Lord with a sincere desire for understanding, however, is going to receive an answer from the Lord in His timing and by His methods. Listen for it!

7. "If then you were raised with Christ, seek those things which are above, where Christ is, sitting at the right hand of God. Set your mind on things above, not on things on the earth" (Colossians 3:1–2). What does it mean to "set your mind on things above"?

....

....

....

....

....

....

....

8. How would such a mindset influence your prayers? How would it influence your overall attitude? How would it influence your reactions to life's surprises?

....

....

....

....

....

....

....

LISTEN FOR OPPORTUNITIES TO GIVE A WITNESS

Finally, look for opportunities to witness for Christ. Every conversation you have with a friend or coworker, every encounter you have with a stranger, and every chance meeting is an opportunity to share God's love. Many people think that giving a witness for the Lord is limited to explaining the plan of salvation. But the reality is that many times your witness to another person will be a reminder of God's love, a word of wisdom from God's Word, or a word of encouragement. Look for ways continually to insert the name of Jesus into your conversations.

At times, the Lord may want you to admonish or to pray for a person. All of those are ways of witnessing to a person that God cares, God loves, God forgives, and God is present. So, as you prepare to meet with a person who is sick, in need, or just stopping by for a friendly visit, be sure to ask the Lord, "What would *You* say to this person if You were meeting with him today?" Then make sure that you listen for the Lord's answer.

Jesus frequently called His disciples to have "eyes to see" and "ears to hear" what God was desiring to do in their midst (see, for example, Matthew 11:15 and 13:9). Those who had ears to hear both heard and understood what the Lord was telling them. This is the goal for all of your listening: a greater understanding of what the Lord is desiring to communicate to you and through you. You are developing eyes to see and ears to hear when you spend time listening to the Lord, praise Him often, continually seek out His presence and work in your life, and look for frequent opportunities to give witness to Him.

9. "But sanctify the Lord God in your hearts, and always be ready to give a defense to everyone who asks you a reason for the hope that is in you, with meekness and fear; having a good conscience, that when they defame you as evildoers, those who revile your good conduct in Christ may be ashamed" (1 Peter 3:15–16). What does it mean to "sanctify the Lord God in your hearts"? How does this influence your prayers?

10. According to these verses, what is involved in witnessing to others about Christ?

TODAY AND TOMORROW

Today: God does speak to me—but I must
first be willing to listen.

Tomorrow: I will practice listening in silence
during my prayer times this week.

CLOSING PRAYER

Jesus, we desire today to be more like You. We choose to wait in Your presence, practice frequent praise throughout the day, and look for ways to see You in the midst of our circumstances. Speak to us and help us to keep our hearts and minds open to hear Your voice. Give us "eyes to see" and "ears to hear" so that we can understand what You are desiring to communicate to us. Let our lives be a witness that draws others to the truth of the gospel.

Notes and
Prayer Requests

Use this space to write any key points, questions, or prayer requests from this week's study.

FAITHFUL GIVING

IN THIS LESSON

Learning: What is the reason for tithing?

Growing: What is considered a "correct" tithe?

The Christian life is intended to be one of generous giving. In fact, one of the most blessed and rewarding aspects of spiritual discipline is giving regularly of our time, talents, and material resources to those in need. The basic understanding of all believers in Christ Jesus is that everything we have received in this life is a gift to us from God. This includes every minute that we live, every ability we possess, every opportunity we are given, every child that we raise, every item of material wealth, and even our abilities to express love and have faith. God gives to us first, and it is out of the abundance of His supply to us that we give.

This concept is referred to as *stewardship*—supervising or taking care of resources entrusted to us by someone else. Jesus addressed the topic of stewardship in His parable of the talents: "A man . . . called his own servants and delivered his goods to them. And to one he gave five talents, to another two, and to another one, to each according to his own ability; and immediately he went on a journey" (Matthew 25:14–15). When the man returned, he rewarded his servants based on the return they had received on his investment.

Financial stewardship has to do with the way in which you use your resources to provide for your needs and for the needs of God's kingdom. Of course, stewardship involves more than your money, because your resources involve more than material goods. Among your resources are your talents, experiences, creative ideas, energy, time, spiritual gifts, and much more. Your resources encompass the total you. God desires to bless all of you and to be directly involved in every area of your life. He wants all of you to be actively involved in His plan for this world.

God has given you all that you have and all of your potential. All that you are and all that you will ever be are His special gifts to you. When it comes to the spiritual discipline of giving, His desire is that you will return to Him all that you are and all that you hope to be. In this manner, stewardship involves all the giving and receiving principles that apply to your relationship with God and your support of God's plan for your life. It implies a caretaker role. A good steward manages the resources of the master with the utmost care and concern.

Every person is a steward of God's gifts, including money and material goods. Therefore, stewardship is something with which all people are involved, whether they recognize it or not. You are a financial steward for your Master and Lord, Jesus Christ. God has a perfect plan for what you are to do with your money and material wealth. He has a plan for blessing you and for you to increase your ability to bless others through the practice of giving.

1. "Our God, we thank You and praise Your glorious name. But who am I, and who are my people, that we should be able to offer so willingly as this? For all things come from You, and of Your own we have given You" (1 Chronicles 29:13–14). What does the writer of these verses suggest about the gifts that God's people offer to Him as sacrifices?

2. According to these verses, from where do all blessings originate? What does this suggest about your obligation to support your local church?

Practice Cheerful Giving

"We love Him because He first loved us" (1 John 4:19). God loved us first, gave to us first, and is the Source of all that we possess in this life. The Lord challenges us to respond to this act by engaging in three specific ways of expressing our faith through giving.

First, we are to be cheerful givers. All too often, Christians have a negative reaction to those who teach about giving. In all likelihood, they also have a negative reaction toward the act of giving! However, we need to remember that giving is commanded by God. Jesus taught, "Give, and it will be given to you: good measure, pressed down, shaken together, and running over will be put into your bosom" (Luke 6:38). He also said, "Freely you have received, freely give" (Matthew 10:8), and, "Sell what you have and give alms; provide yourselves money bags which do not grow old, a treasure in the heavens that does not fail" (Luke 12:33).

Giving is a means of activating our individual faith. It is a means of meeting needs in the world. It is also a means of bringing about an abundant return for God's kingdom. When we catch a glimpse of the great rewards that are associated with our giving, we cannot help but be cheerful!

Note that we do not give to the Lord to "pay back God" for anything. God's gift of salvation to us is a free act motivated solely by His love for us. The same is true of all God's gifts: He gives to us because we are His beloved children. Our giving to God is simply a means that He uses to meet the needs of others and cause a great abundance of joy and blessings to come our way. Jesus said, "For with the same measure that you use, it will be measured back to you" (Luke 6:38). God multiplies what we give to others in ways that we cannot understand . . . but in which we surely can receive!

3. "So let each one give as he purposes in his heart, not grudgingly or of necessity; for God loves a cheerful giver" (2 Corinthians

9:7). What tends to be your attitude when you give of your income to the Lord's work? Explain.

....

....

....

....

....

....

....

....

4. Why does Paul command us to give as we "purpose in our heart"? Why does he not just provide a formula for giving?

....

....

....

....

....

....

....

....

PRACTICE CONSISTENT GIVING

Second, we are to be consistent givers. The standard that God sets for our giving is a *tithe* (one-tenth) of what we receive. In the Old Testament, God designed the system specifically to meet the needs or the religious, economic, and political systems of ancient Israel. Each of the twelve tribes of Israel, with the exception of the tribe of Levi, were to give a tenth of all their produce, flocks, and cattle to support the Levis. In turn, the Levites gave a tenth of those resources to support the work of the priests (see Leviticus 27:30–33 and Numbers

18:21–28). God also commanded tithes to be given to support those in need (see Deuteronomy 26:12–13).

This system implies that our giving is not to be sporadic or scattered but consistent and focused. As we receive, we are to regularly give a tenth back to God's work. Furthermore, we are to give to the place where we participate in the worship of the Lord. The tithe is *not* intended for a charitable organization but for a work that bears the Lord's name. It is to further the work of the Lord, which is the spreading of the gospel and the teaching of God's Word.

As God said through the prophet Malachi, "Will a man rob God? Yet you have robbed Me! But you say, 'In what way have we robbed You?' In tithes and offerings. You are cursed with a curse, for you have robbed Me, even this whole nation. Bring all the tithes into the storehouse, that there may be food in My house, and try Me now in this . . . if I will not open for you the windows of heaven and pour out for you such blessing that there will not be room enough to receive it. And I will rebuke the devourer for your sakes, so that he will not destroy the fruit of your ground, nor shall the vine fail to bear fruit for you in the field" (Malachi 3:8–11).

God draws a clear line. Those who fail to give according to His commandments are *not blessed*, while those who do give tithes and offerings *are blessed*. Furthermore, these commandments are still relevant to us today. Tithing was not just for Old Testament times. In the Gospels, we do not find Jesus teaching about tithing for the sole reason that the people were already tithing! Tithing was deeply ingrained in the fabric of that society, so there was no reason for Him to preach about something the people were already doing.

In fact, the deeply religious Pharisees were tithing the herbs that grew in their gardens. Jesus did not criticize their tithing. Rather, He approved of their tithing but said they were to place greater importance on bigger issues such as God's justice and God's love. As He said, "You tithe mint and rue and all manner of herbs, and pass by justice and the love of God. These you ought to have done, without leaving the others undone" (Luke 11:42). Jesus also taught about giving to the needy (see Matthew 25:37–40) and about sacrificial giving (see Mark 12:41–44).

5. "Will a man rob God? Yet you have robbed Me! But you say, 'In what way have we robbed You?' In tithes and offerings" (Malachi 3:8). What is God's view of a person who fails to tithe? What are the results of consistently giving back to God?

6. "Honor the LORD with your possessions, and with the firstfruits of all your increase; so your barns will be filled with plenty, and your vats will overflow with new wine" (Proverbs 3:9–10). What does it mean to "honor" God with your possessions?

Practice Generous Giving

Third, we are to be generous givers. In the book of Acts, we find that the first-century Christians were generous givers. They tithed to the storehouse of the Lord, and in some cases they sacrificed all they had for the benefit of their brothers and sisters in Christ. As a result, "there [was not] anyone among them who lacked; for all who were possessors of lands or houses sold them, and brought the proceeds of the things that were sold" (Acts 4:34–35).

In Paul's letter to the Romans, he described a spiritual gift of giving and admonished those who had this gift to give with liberality. "Having then gifts differing according to the grace that is given to us, let us use them . . . he who exhorts, in exhortation; he who gives, with liberality; he who leads, with diligence; he who shows mercy, with cheerfulness" (12:6, 8). Those who are called to such a ministry go beyond the giving of tithes and offerings. All of us, however, are challenged to give with generosity—to go above and beyond the tithe and give generous offerings. The degree to which we give is the degree to which we receive.

7. "He who sows sparingly will also reap sparingly, and he who sows bountifully will also reap bountifully" (2 Corinthians 9:6). How is tithing similar to sowing seed in a garden?

8. What determines God's blessing—the amount given or the spirit of the giver?

....

....

....

....

....

....

....

....

....

....

....

EXPRESS YOUR TRUST IN GOD

Fourth, we are to view our giving as a direct expression of our trust in God. Giving is a sign of our willingness to let go of the control of our life and our material wellbeing and let God direct us, use us, and bless us as He desires. As the psalmist wrote, "Oh, taste and see that the LORD is good; blessed is the man who trusts in Him! Oh, fear the LORD, you His saints! There is no want to those who fear Him. The young lions lack and suffer hunger; But those who seek the LORD shall not lack any good thing" (Psalm 34:8–10).

The promise of God to you as His beloved child is that He "shall supply all your need according to His riches in glory by Christ Jesus" (Philippians 4:19). So, are you willing to trust God today with your giving? Are you willing to trust Him to take care of you and to meet all of your material needs? It will take discipline of your will to become a cheerful, consistent, and generous giver. However, your giving is a key to releasing the blessings of God into your life. It is vitally linked to your ability to trust God and to your ability to grow spiritually.

9. "And let us not grow weary while doing good, for in due season we shall reap if we do not lose heart" (Galatians 6:9). What might cause a person to "grow weary" or "lose heart" when it comes to giving? What can you do to guard against this?

....
....
....
....
....
....
....

10. What are some of the blessings you have reaped when you have given generously?

....
....
....
....
....
....
....

TODAY AND TOMORROW

Today: The Lord wants me to give back to Him some of the blessings that He has given me.

Tomorrow: I will begin a regular schedule of tithing this month and will work on doing it cheerfully.

CLOSING PRAYER

Heavenly Father, give us the willingness today to take an inventory of our lives. Help us to uncover where our true treasure lies—where we are spending our time, energy, and resources. Reveal any priorities that we have put above You, especially in the area of our finances. Help us to be willing and cheerful givers who are good stewards of the gifts You have bestowed on us. Help us to view our gift-giving as an important work to further the gospel and Your kingdom.

Notes and Prayer Requests

Use this space to write any key points, questions, or prayer requests from this week's study.

INVOLVEMENT IN MINISTRY

IN THIS LESSON

Learning: Is it really that important to go to church?

Growing: What difference can I make in a local church?

One of the most important spiritual disciplines you can develop is faithful involvement with other believers. I am always amazed when a Christian tells me, "Oh, I don't go to church very often. I would rather stay at home and watch sermons online or listen to Christian television and radio programs." Others reluctantly admit to me, "I only go to church when I can work it into my family schedule," or, "I go to church *as often as I can*," which usually means not often.

I certainly am all in favor of Christian television and radio ministries. But I also know they are no substitute for regular attendance and faithful involvement in the worship services, ministry outreaches, and educational programs at church. Of course, this is not always possible for every person. Many people are bedridden or deal with other afflictions that prevent them from being able to get to a local church on a regular basis. The more recent global pandemic has also led many churches to close their doors temporarily and meet online.

However, the spiritual discipline of engaging with other believers to worship and serve God together—in whatever form it must take—still holds true. In the book of Acts, we read how from the very start of the church, the believers gathered together in fellowship. "Then those who gladly received [Peter's] word were baptized; and that day about three thousand souls were added to them. And they continued steadfastly in the apostles' doctrine and fellowship, in the breaking of bread, and in prayers.... So continuing daily with one accord in the temple, and breaking bread from house to house, they ate their food with gladness and simplicity of heart, praising God and having favor with all the people" (Acts 2:41–42, 46–47).

The author of Hebrews also encourages each of us to engage in Christian fellowship when he writes, "Let us consider one another in order to stir up love and good works, not forsaking the assembling of ourselves together, as is the manner of some, but exhorting one another, and so much the more as you see the Day approaching" (Hebrews 10:24–25).

1. What does it mean to "stir up love and good works"? Why do such things need to be stirred up with believers in Christ?

2. According to these verses, why is it necessary for other Christians to be involved in that process? What role does the church play?

....

....

....

....

....

....

....

....

....

....

....

....

....

BE ENGAGED IN THE BODY OF CHRIST

No Christian has ever been called to "go it alone" in his or her faith. We need one another. The church was designed from the beginning to function as the living body of Christ on the earth after the Lord's resurrection and ascension. As the apostle Paul wrote, "For as we have many members in one body, but all the members do not have the same function, so we, being many, are one body in Christ, and individually members of one another. Having then gifts differing according to the grace that is given to us, let us use them" (Romans 12:4–6).

Part of the reason that we need to be in regular fellowship with other believers is so that we can receive the benefit of their spiritual gifts and, in turn, give our spiritual gifts to the body of Christ. We individually are made stronger as we both receive and give. Simultaneously, the church to which we belong is made stronger and more effective as a whole.

3. Why does Paul use the analogy of the human body to describe the church? How does this illustrate the importance of regular church involvement?

....

....

....

....

....

....

....

....

....

....

4. What is the purpose of spiritual gifts? Where are they to be used?

....

....

....

....

....

....

....

....

....

....

MINISTER TO OTHER BELIEVERS

Jesus made it clear that our foremost ministry to other believers is to love them. As He said to His disciples, "This is My commandment, that you love one another as I have loved you" (John 15:12). Paul echoed this command: "Be imitators of God as dear children.

And walk in love, as Christ also has loved us and given Himself for us" (Ephesians 5:1-2).

The New Testament writers identified several ways in which we are called to show love to one another within the body of Christ. Paul wrote the following to the Colossian believers: "Let the peace of God rule in your hearts, to which also you were called in one body; and be thankful. Let the word of Christ dwell in you richly in all wisdom, teaching and admonishing one another in psalms and hymns and spiritual songs, singing with grace in your hearts to the Lord. And whatever you do in word or deed, do all in the name of the Lord Jesus, giving thanks to God the Father through Him" (Colossians 3:15-17).

John wrote the following: "Beloved, let us love one another, for love is of God; and everyone who loves is born of God and knows God. He who does not love does not know God, for God is love. In this the love of God was manifested toward us, that God has sent His only begotten Son into the world, that we might live through Him. In this is love, not that we loved God, but that He loved us and sent His Son to be the propitiation for our sins. Beloved, if God so loved us, we also ought to love one another" (1 John 4:7-11).

Peter wrote these words about love in the body of Christ: "But the end of all things is at hand; therefore be serious and watchful in your prayers. And above all things have fervent love for one another, for 'love will cover a multitude of sins.' Be hospitable to one another without grumbling. As each one has received a gift, minister it to one another, as good stewards of the manifold grace of God" (1 Peter 4:7-10).

As members of the body of Christ, we are to love our fellow believers by praying for one another (see James 5:16), speaking well of one another (see James 4:11), being truthful and willing to even admonish one another in love (see Romans 15:14), being hospitable to one another (see 1 Timothy 3:2), comforting one another (see 1 Thessalonians 5:11), pursuing the common good (see 1 Thessalonians 5:15), encouraging and building up one another (see 1 Corinthians 14:26), and blessing one another (see 1 Peter 3:8-9).

5. What are some ways that you are actively praying for your fellow believers in Christ, speaking well of them, and practicing hospitality toward them?

....

....

....

....

....

....

6. What are some ways that you are actively comforting your fellow believers in Christ, encouraging them and building them up, and blessing them with your service?

....

....

....

....

....

....

MINISTER TO THOSE OUTSIDE THE CHURCH

Along with serving others in the body of Christ, we are to be involved in active ministry to those who do not know the Lord. In the Gospels, we read how Jesus sent out His disciples two by two. He gave them power and authority over all demons and power to cure diseases. He told them to preach the kingdom of God where they went and heal the sick (see Luke 9:1–2).

On another occasion, Jesus sent out seventy of His disciples, again two by two, and said to them, "The harvest truly is great, but the laborers are few; therefore pray the Lord of the harvest to send out laborers into His harvest.... Heal the sick there, and say to them, 'The kingdom of God has come near to you'" (Luke 10:2, 9). If we desire to be followers of Jesus today, we must acknowledge that He is sending us out today as well. He is saying the same things to us: we are to heal the sick and proclaim the kingdom of God.

We live in a chaotic world filled with anxiety and fear. Events arise that expose the vulnerabilities and limitations of our government, medical science, and the global economy. But through it all, we see that Jesus remains an unfailing and unshakable source of hope and security. The people in our world need to experience that same hope. They need a reason to keep on going—a message that lifts them from the despair of their circumstances. The only way they will receive this message—the hope of salvation—is through believers in Christ.

Remember Jesus' words to His disciples before He was taken up into heaven: "Go therefore and make disciples of all the nations, baptizing them in the name of the Father and of the Son and of the Holy Spirit, teaching them to observe all things that I have commanded you; and lo, I am with you always, even to the end of the age" (Matthew 28:19-20). We are all "ambassadors for Christ" in this world with the mission of reaching the lost (2 Corinthians 5:20).

7. "Go into all the world and preach the gospel to every creature. He who believes and is baptized will be saved; but he who does not believe will be condemned" (Mark 16:15-16). Why is it so critical for followers of Christ to share the message of the gospel?

8. "Pure and undefiled religion before God and the Father is this: to visit orphans and widows in their trouble, and to keep oneself unspotted from the world" (James 1:27). What does this verse say about the importance of ministering to those in need—whether they are inside or outside of the church?

....

....

....

....

....

....

....

....

TAKE ON THE MINISTRY OF CHRIST

Jesus used the words of Isaiah to describe His ministry on earth: "The Spirit of the LORD is upon Me, because He has anointed Me to preach the gospel to the poor; He has sent Me to heal the brokenhearted, to proclaim liberty to the captives and recovery of sight to the blind, to set at liberty those who are oppressed; to proclaim the acceptable year of the LORD" (Luke 4:18–19).

Remember, you are never called to *go it alone* in your faith. You are never called to *go it alone* in your ministry to others. Just as Jesus sent out His disciples *two by two*, He desires for you to partner with other believers in sharing both the burden and the benefits of ministering in His name. As Christ said, "If two of you agree on earth concerning anything that they ask, it will be done for them by My Father in heaven. For where two or three are gathered together in My name, I am there in the midst of them" (Matthew 18:19–20).

There is synergy that takes place when two or more believers stand together for a common mission, purpose, or cause. Paul understood this truth when he encouraged the Corinthian believers to "[let] there be no divisions among you, but . . . be perfectly joined together in the same mind and in the same judgment" (1 Corinthians 1:10). He likewise encouraged the Philippian believers to "stand fast in *one spirit*, with one mind striving together for the faith of the gospel" (Philippians 1:27).

In the book of Revelation, the disciple John recorded again and again these four convicting words of Jesus: "I know your works" (see Revelation 2:2, 9, 19). What we do as the body of Christ—as unto the Lord, unto one another, and unto the lost—matters deeply to God. For this reason, we need to make our actions count!

9. "The righteous will answer Him, saying, 'Lord, when did we see You hungry and feed You, or thirsty and give You drink? When did we see You a stranger and take You in, or naked and clothe You? Or when did we see You sick, or in prison, and come to You?' And the King will answer and say to them, 'Assuredly, I say to you, inasmuch as you did it to one of the least of these My brethren, you did it to Me'" (Matthew 25:37-40). Why does Jesus say that we are ministering to Him when we minister to others? What does this imply about your involvement in a local church?

10. "If one member suffers, all the members suffer with it; or if one member is honored, all the members rejoice with it. Now you are the body of Christ, and members individually" (1 Corinthians 12:26–27). Why is it important for all Christians to be involved regularly with a local church? What happens when one part of the body becomes separated?

TODAY AND TOMORROW

Today: I am part of Christ's body, and therefore I must remain connected to other parts of His body.

Tomorrow: I will become involved in the ministries of my local church on a regular basis.

CLOSING PRAYER

Heavenly Father, we invite You to work in our midst in the body of Christ. We want to be a dynamic force for You in our neighborhoods, our cities, and all across our nation. We know that just a handful of dedicated believers—indwelt by the Holy Spirit, living in obedience, committed to the Great Commission—can have a huge impact on the world. We know there is no limitation to what You can do when we willingly submit to You in service. Use us today, we pray.

NOTES AND PRAYER REQUESTS

Use this space to write any key points, questions, or prayer requests from this week's study.

FOUR BASICS OF SPIRITUAL GROWTH

IN THIS LESSON

Learning: If God loves me, then why do I have to suffer?

Growing: How can I learn from those who are wise?

As we established earlier in this study, as followers of Christ, we are all *commanded* to grow spiritually. We are admonished to practice spiritual disciplines and to mature in our faith. Peter said, "Grow in the grace and knowledge of our Lord and Savior Jesus Christ" (2 Peter 3:18). This is not a nice statement of encouragement or advice. It is a direct command from the Lord.

None of us automatically grows spiritually. Each of us must *choose* to grow . . . and we must choose to *continue* to grow. We can never be satisfied with our current level of spiritual strength but should view our spiritual growth as an ongoing process. We must always seek to become stronger, more mature, and more effective for the Lord. In the Bible, we find four keys that are prerequisites to this kind of growth, regardless of how mature we might be in the Lord.

BE READY TO FACE FAILURES

Most of us try to dismiss, sidestep, or justify our faults and failures. We sometimes try to take the easy way out, saying, "That is just the way I am," or, "That is just the way I was raised." The fact is that most of us are *not* just the way that God wants us to be. Before the basic spiritual disciplines can be effective, maturing us into the likeness of Christ Jesus, we must face our faults and failures, take responsibility for them, and go to God with them.

Is there an area in your life where you have experienced repeated failures? Can you point to certain faults that you seem to have struggled against all your life? Let me assure you, God has a way for those failures to be turned into victories and strengths. God has a great desire to see you made whole, and He will continue to pursue the faults and failures that fragment you and cause you to be dysfunctional, uneasy, or deeply frustrated. He will continue to move against any obstacle that stands in the way of your wholeness or intimacy with Him.

For this reason, the first step you must take toward spiritual growth is to *own up to your failures, flaws, and faults*. Stop blaming others and assume responsibility for those shortcomings. Confess to God, "I have brought myself to the place where I am today. I am the one who has allowed this past to continue to be my present."

True repentance means moving in the opposite direction from past sins. It is an act of the will, empowered by the Holy Spirit within you, to change from your wicked ways, evil attitudes, hurtful words, and wrong behaviors. Of course, to reach this place of repentance, you first must be willing to own up to those things that need to be changed. If the spiritual disciplines you practice are going to be effective, you must recognize some things about your life need healing. You are responsible for using your will and faith to bring about positive changes.

1. "Therefore we also, since we are surrounded by so great a cloud of witnesses, let us lay aside every weight, and the sin which so easily ensnares us, and let us run with endurance the race that is set before us" (Hebrews 12:1). What is the race that has been "set before" you? In what areas do you need more endurance?

2. What sins frequently ensnare you in your life? What weights are slowing you down? What will you do this week to seek to get rid of those things?

Receive Godly Counsel

All followers of Christ, regardless of the degree of spiritual strength and maturity they possess, can benefit from wise counsel that is couched in love, forgiveness, and confidentiality. God has placed Christian brothers and sisters in your life to encourage you, admonish you, teach you, and give you godly counsel regarding God's plan for your life. Avail yourself of their help!

In order to benefit from such wise counsel, you must choose to be transparent and vulnerable emotionally with the other person. You must choose to be candid, forthcoming, and truthful about your own life, desires, and motivations. You have to face up to the fact that you do not know fully all that God wants you to know and that you need greater wisdom. This wisdom can come only as you share your life in Christ.

God's Word must always be the basis for wise counsel. Any advice you receive must flow from God's Word and be echoed by God's Word. If you truly desire to grow to full spiritual maturity in Christ Jesus, you need to avail yourself of the wisdom others can offer to you.

3. "So then, my beloved brethren, let every man be swift to hear, slow to speak, slow to wrath; for the wrath of man does not produce the righteousness of God" (James 1:19–20). What is involved in being "swift to hear"? Why must you be "slow to speak"?

4. What role does wrath play in one's willingness to hear wise counsel? How does wrath in an individual keep God's righteousness from being produced?

....

....

....

....

....

....

....

....

....

....

....

....

....

....

....

....

REFLECT ON GOD'S WORK

The Bible commands you to trust God to meet your *daily* needs and walk fully in the present moment of your existence. At the same time, there are numerous instances in God's Word in which people were called to reflect on God's goodness to them. They were given a glimpse of the eternal work He was doing, both in the world of their day and throughout the ages.

As you learn about the ways in which God has worked in the lives of others in the past, you will gain a greater understanding of how God is presently at work in your life. You can learn a great deal by hearing and reflecting on the way God is working in the lives of other Christians today. These include those whom you recognize as being more mature in Christ Jesus.

If you are to benefit fully from practicing spiritual disciplines, you need to be able to see your life in the broader context of what God is doing and what He desires to do in the world. You must observe how your life meshes with the lives of others in your family, your church, and your community. You must also gain an understanding that what the Lord desires to do *in* you is related to what He desires ultimately to do *through* you.

5. "Now, therefore, you are no longer strangers and foreigners, but fellow citizens with the saints and members of the household of God, having been built on the foundation of the apostles and prophets, Jesus Christ Himself being the chief cornerstone, in whom the whole building, being fitted together, grows into a holy temple in the Lord, in whom you also are being built together for a dwelling place of God in the Spirit" (Ephesians 2:19–22). What does it mean to you to be a member of the household of God?

6. What have you learned from God's involvement in the lives of other Christians? In what ways are you blessed by God's work in those who have gone before?

....

....

....

....

....

....

....

....

....

....

....

....

RESPOND PROPERLY TO TRIALS

Believers in Christ who practice the spiritual disciplines and are growing spiritually are naturally going to face tests and trials in this life. Many people believe that God should spare Christians from all negative experiences. But the reality is that God frequently uses trials and tests for our benefit. They become our opportunity to learn more about God's methods, purposes, and perfect plan. They serve as our "school" for learning how to grow stronger in faith.

For this reason, If you are practicing the spiritual disciplines, you need to be equipped to face the trials that will come your way. Rather than run from them, ask God why He has allowed them to come into your life. Look for the lesson that He desires to teach you or the character trait He desires to develop or strengthen. God knows all about the tests you are experiencing, and He has allowed them to come into your life for a purpose. So ask Him to reveal that purpose to you. Ask Him to help you trust Him to bring you through in a way that results in glory to Him.

At the same time, ask the Lord if the trials you are experiencing are a chastening from Him. The Lord only chastens those whom He loves and desires to perfect. So ask the Lord, "Is there something in my life that You want me to change?" If the answer is *yes*, act quickly to obey the Lord's command or to confess the sin that is holding you back from spiritual growth.

7. "Beloved, do not think it strange concerning the fiery trial which is to try you, as though some strange thing happened to you; but rejoice to the extent that you partake of Christ's sufferings, that when His glory is revealed, you may also be glad with exceeding joy" (1 Peter 4:12-13). When have you gone through a "fiery trial" that strengthened your character? What trials might God be using right now to make you more like Christ?

....

....

....

....

....

....

....

8. In what are you called to rejoice as you face trials? How can such rejoicing make a trial more helpful to your spiritual growth?

....

....

....

....

....

....

....

....

WALK IN STEP WITH THE SPIRIT

We must never lose sight of the fact that we are in relationship with a *holy* God. God manifests no darkness, no shadow of turning, and no tolerance for evil or deceit. For us to approach God, we must thus be in a state of forgiveness, which is only made possible as we face up to our sin, seek God's forgiveness, and choose to live in His righteousness. This is a daily decision that each of us must make—a daily decision to confess our sin, a daily receiving of His forgiveness, and a daily desire to walk in the paths that the Holy Spirit reveals to us.

Those who refuse to face their faults and failures cannot grow spiritually. Those who refuse to receive godly counsel cannot grow into great spiritual maturity. Those who do not see their lives in the broader context of God's plan for all humankind cannot know how to employ spiritual strength and power. Those who are unwilling to face life's trials and troubles with a reliance on God cannot become strong spiritually. Those who are unwilling to be chastened by the Lord cannot grow toward perfection in Christ Jesus.

The apostle Paul wrote, "Those who are Christ's have crucified the flesh with its passions and desires. If we live in the Spirit, let us also walk in the Spirit" (Galatians 5:24-25). Each of us must be certain that we are walking in step with the Spirit—which means facing our faults, confessing our sins, receiving godly counsel, seeking God's "big picture" for our lives, trusting in Him regardless of circumstances, and yielding to His chastening.

As a follower of Christ, you can read your Bible daily, communicate with the Lord often in prayer, attend church regularly, be involved in outreach ministry, and give faithfully. But unless you are willing to change, to grow, to be shaped by God, and then to be used in whatever manner that He desires, these disciplines will not yield their maximum benefit in your life. A total submission of your life to God's remolding and remaking of you is required.

9. "My son, do not despise the chastening of the LORD, nor be dis-couraged when you are rebuked by Him; for whom the LORD loves He chastens, and scourges every son whom He receives'" (Hebrews 12:5–6). What does it mean to be a son of God? What privileges does that bring? What responsibilities does it require?

10. What is a *scourge*? Why would God choose to use a scourge on a son whom He loves? What is His purpose for this chastening?

TODAY AND TOMORROW

Today: God uses other Christians, as well as circumstances, to make me more like Christ.

Tomorrow: I will ask the Lord this week to teach me through other Christians and through life's circumstances.

CLOSING PRAYER

Lord, we commit to following Your command to grow spiritually. We choose to grow . . . and choose to continue to grow in our faith. Thank You for desiring to have a relationship with each of us. We want to grow in our understanding of You. Help us, we pray, to be ready to face failures and learn from them. Help us to be open to receiving godly counsel. Help us to reflect on the work You are doing in our lives and respond in the way You want to trials—so that we can learn the lessons from them that You want to teach us. Help us to walk in step with Your Spirit.

NOTES AND PRAYER REQUESTS

Use this space to write any key points, questions, or prayer requests from this week's study.

Ten Hallmarks of Spiritual Strength

Learning: What distinguishes a mature Christian from an immature Christian?

Growing: How can I tell if I am making progress?

From my years of pastoring, I have concluded there are ten hallmarks that routinely appear in those who are spiritually strong. As you read through these attributes and study them, I encourage you to evaluate your own life and refrain from judging others. These attributes may not be present in everyone in equal amounts, but they are the marks of those who are spiritually healthy and mature. They are the attributes of those who have grown to a deep level of intimacy with God and who routinely experience God's presence and power in their lives.

A Hunger for God and a Desire to Know His Truth

The first hallmark of those who are spiritually mature is a hunger for the things of God. This hunger is what has led these individuals to develop spiritual disciplines and mature in Christ. They are not content with knowing God in an objective way as Creator, Savior, or almighty God. Rather, they desire to know Him as *Lord*, to develop an intimate relationship with Him, to know what He desires of them, and to experience His presence on a daily basis. They want to know God in all His fullness—Father, Son, and Holy Spirit. They desire to recognize and respond immediately to the prompting of the Holy Spirit in whatever way that He may lead them.

The second hallmark of those who are spiritually mature is a desire to know God's Word and apply it to their lives. These individuals know what the Bible has to say. They know the meaning of the Scriptures and consider God's Word to be the ultimate authority in helping them make daily decisions and eternally significant choices. They view the Word of God as "living and powerful, and sharper than any two-edged sword, piercing even to the division of soul and spirit, and of joints and marrow" (Hebrews 4:12).

1. "As the deer pants for the water brooks, so pants my soul for You, O God. My soul thirsts for God, for the living God" (Psalm 42:1–2). When have you experienced a deep thirst for God's presence? How did you satisfy that thirst?

2. "Teach me, O Lord, the way of Your statutes, and I shall keep it to the end. Give me understanding, and I shall keep Your law; indeed, I shall observe it with my whole heart" (Psalm 119:33–34). What is God's role in spiritual growth? What is your role?

....

....

....

....

....

....

....

....

....

....

....

....

A Desire for God's Will to Be Done and Love for Others

The third hallmark of those who are spiritually mature is a desire for God's will to be done on earth. The Bible teaches that believers in Christ are *in* this world but are not to be *of* this world (see John 17:16). In this world, we must abide by natural laws, live within the constraints of human-made laws, and provide for ourselves. But we are not to have the same desires and lusts the world exhibits. We are not to have the same dreams, goals, or hopes. Rather, we are to desire with our whole heart that God's will be done on this earth. As we pray in the Lord's Prayer, "Your kingdom come. Your will be done on earth as it is in heaven" (Matthew 6:10).

The fourth hallmark of those who are spiritually mature is a great love for others. Mature Christians are able to express their love and have a desire to extend that love to an ever-widening circle of people. They have little concern with appearances, status, or personal reputation—rather, their foremost concern is with expressing God's love to sinners and to any person in need. They have an ever-growing desire to reach out, to touch, to speak, to share, to listen, and to be used by God to shower His love on those who are hurting.

3. "Do not love the world or the things in the world. If anyone loves the world, the love of the Father is not in him. For all that is in the world—the lust of the flesh, the lust of the eyes, and the pride of life—is not of the Father but is of the world" (1 John 2:15-16). Why are love of the world and love of your heavenly Father mutually exclusive?

4. "If someone says, 'I love God,' and hates his brother, he is a liar; for he who does not love his brother whom he has seen, how can he love God whom he has not seen? And this commandment we have from Him: that he who loves God must love his brother also" (1 John 4:20-21). Why is it impossible to love God and have hatred in your heart toward another person at the same time?

....

....

....

....

....

....

....

....

....

....

....

....

....

No Tolerance for Evil but a Quickness to Forgive

The fifth hallmark of those who are spiritually mature is refusal to tolerate evil in any form. They are able to discern evil, recognize sin, and have an abhorrence for all that is contrary to God's goodness, grace, mercy, love, and forgiveness. Spiritually mature Christians are not judgmental of people but of actions and words. They understand that as believers in Christ, they are called to judge deeds and judge right from wrong (see 1 Peter 4:17). They have a desire to remove themselves as far as possible from activities and situations that give rise to sin.

131

The sixth hallmark of those who are spiritually mature is a readiness to immediately forgive those who offend, hurt, or reject them. They harbor no resentment and are quick to make apologies, make amends, and settle disputes peacefully. They do not compromise with evil or have a desire to be yoked with nonbelievers. Instead, they want to live in peace with others and be free of bitterness and feelings of revenge toward others.

5. "By this you know the Spirit of God: Every spirit that confesses that Jesus Christ has come in the flesh is of God, and every spirit that does not confess that Jesus Christ has come in the flesh is not of God" (1 John 4:2–3). What are examples of false teachings that are popular today? How do you know these to be false?

6. "But love your enemies, do good, and lend, hoping for nothing in return; and your reward will be great, and you will be sons of the Most High. For He is kind to the unthankful and evil.

Therefore be merciful, just as your Father also is merciful" What should your mindset be when doing good? How does this reflect Christ's nature?

....

....

....

....

....

....

....

....

....

....

....

READY TO OBEY WITH GREAT FAITH

The seventh hallmark of those who are spiritually mature is a quickness to act when they receive a command from the Holy Spirit. When they feel convicted of sin, they are quick to confess it, seek God's forgiveness, and change their ways. Spiritually mature Christians have a deep desire to do God's will. They long to hear God speak to them, and when He does, they respond enthusiastically and immediately, with full effort given to whatever the Lord commands.

The eighth hallmark of those who are spiritually mature is a willingness to act with great faith. Every person has been given a measure of faith (see Romans 12:3). But not every believer has developed the same degree of faith. Faith is intended to be used and to be exercised. The more a person uses his or her faith, the stronger it grows. The Bible speaks of varying degrees of faith—from little faith (see Matthew 14:31) to great faith (see Matthew 15:28). Mature believers develop and use their faith with the goal of having *great* faith.

7. "Therefore whoever hears these sayings of Mine, and does them, I will liken him to a wise man who built his house on the rock: and the rain descended, the floods came, and the winds blew and beat on that house; and it did not fall, for it was founded on the rock" (Matthew 7:24–25). In what ways is a house more secure if it is built on solid rock rather than on sand? How is this a picture of building your life on God's Word?

....

....

....

....

....

....

....

....

....

8. "When [Peter] saw that the wind was boisterous, he was afraid; and beginning to sink he cried out, saying, 'Lord, save me!' And immediately Jesus stretched out His hand and caught him, and said to him, 'O you of little faith, why did you doubt?'" (Matthew 14:30–31). Peter had been walking on the water in these verses. In what way was his faith too small? How might it have been greater?

....

....

....

....

....

....

....

....

....

A SOFT HEART AND DEEP LOVE FOR GOD

The ninth hallmark of those who are spiritually mature is a soft heart toward those in need. They are tender and sensitive to those who are hurting, and they desire to respond in ways that are appropriate and bring glory to God. Spiritually mature Christians have a strong desire to see sinners receive Christ as their Savior. They are committed to help in whatever way they can to see the practical, emotional, and spiritual needs of others are met.

The tenth hallmark of those who are spiritually mature is a deep love for God. Those who are spiritually mature have an abiding love for God. They recognize God as their loving, merciful, patient heavenly Father—a Father who can be trusted to provide, give wisdom, be present always, bestow blessings, and give unconditional love. They understand the truth of Paul's words when he said, "You did not receive the spirit of bondage again to fear, but you received the Spirit of adoption by whom we cry out, 'Abba, Father'" (Romans 8:15).

9. "Rejoice with those who rejoice, and weep with those who weep. Be of the same mind toward one another. Do not set your mind on high things, but associate with the humble. Do not be wise in your own opinion" (Romans 12:15-16). When has someone rejoiced with you or wept with you? How did that demonstrate the love of God to you?

10. "There is no fear in love; but perfect love casts out fear, because fear involves torment. But he who fears has not been made perfect in love. We love Him because He first loved us" (1 John 4:18-19). How does God love you? What sort of love best mirrors His love?

THE BASICS NEVER CHANGE

Every coach knows that when a team gets into trouble, it is not the time to introduce new plays or change the overall strategy. Rather, it is the time to return to the basics and reinforce the tried-and-true drills and practices. The same is true spiritually. Through the ages, Christians have known that when they practice basic spiritual disciplines—reading God's Word daily, praying often, giving faithfully, attending church regularly, staying active in outreach ministries—they are much more likely to hear from God, experience His love, grow in their talents, and receive blessings beyond anything they had imagined (see Ephesians 3:20).

We never grow beyond our need for the basics. They are the foundation on which all other aspects of our Christian life are built. They are the disciplines that need to become deeply ingrained habits in us. So, consider today in which area of spiritual discipline you find yourself lacking. Make the development of that particular discipline a priority in your life. Then see what God will do in you, through you, and for you. For it is as you practice the basics—regularly, consistently, and with perseverance—that you will grow and become strong in the Lord.

TODAY AND TOMORROW

Today: To become a mature believer, I must always be working on the basic areas of discipline.

Tomorrow: I will continue in the coming weeks to maintain the disciplines that I have begun.

CLOSING PRAYER

Heavenly Father, we have such a long way to grow spiritually. Thank You for Your continual guidance as You lead us on the path of maturing in our faith. We desire to possess all the hallmarks that indicate we are spiritually strong. Help us to have a hunger for You and a desire to know Your truth. Let our goal be to see Your will done on earth as we love and serve others. We pray that we will never tolerate evil or give the enemy a foothold in our lives. Enable us to be quick to forgive, ready to obey you, and always trusting in Your plans. Soften our hearts today so that we can have the heart You have for people as we seek to show them Your love.

Notes and Prayer Requests

Use this space to write any key points, questions, or prayer requests from this week's study.

LIFE'S NUMBER-ONE PRIORITY

IN THIS LESSON

Learning: What should be the first priority in my life?

Growing: How will my life change when I set spending time with Jesus as my number-one priority?

How many decisions have you made today? Take a moment to think about it. What are some of the larger decisions you have made in the last twenty-four hours? How many decisions are you typically confronted with over the course of a given week?

Life is filled with decisions. For that reason, our lives will often be filled with tension. Decisions have a way of exposing what is tugging at us in different areas of our lives. There are interests and desires that pull at us from one direction, and interests and desires that pull at us from a different direction—and we have to decide which of those tugs to follow. The main area in which we feel this tension is between what we would *like* to do and what we *should* do. We feel pulled between those things we prefer to do and those things we are supposed to do.

This is especially true when it comes to spiritual disciplines. Every day, you are going to feel tension when it comes to practicing the disciplines that we have explored in this study. You know deep in your heart that you *should* set aside time and make efforts to invest in these practices—to invest in your spiritual life and your spiritual connection with God. But you also have other things you would like to do. So you are going to feel the tension between those two poles.

Many Christians respond to that tension by trying to gut their way through it. They grudgingly read their Bibles, set aside time to pray, invest in encountering God, and so on. It is like eating vegetables for them. They tell themselves, *"I know it's healthy for me, so I'm going to grit my teeth and get it done."* But this never works in the long run. You cannot build your spiritual life on so shaky a foundation.

Thankfully, there is a simple way to address this tension. The solution is to delve into the root issue of your priorities in life. This is what we will explore together in this final lesson.

1. When do you tend to feel tension between what you would like to do and what you know that you should do?

....

....

....

....

....

....

....

....

2. Which of the spiritual disciplines are you currently trying to force yourself to enjoy or practice right now? How is it going?

....

....

....

....

....

....

....

....

....

....

....

....

....

WE ALL HAVE PRIORITIES IN LIFE

Every person has a cascading series of priorities that govern their lives. Whether or not we understand those priorities is a different question. But they are there—and they impact just about every choice we make. A *priority* is simply an ideal that takes precedence over all others. When you rank your preferences in a certain area of life, you can quickly discover your priorities by seeing what rises to the top of that list. This does not mean the other things on your list are un-important. But your priority is of *first importance*.

It is necessary to have different priorities that correspond to the different areas of our lives. For instance, we have priorities when it comes to finances. We have priorities when it comes to our relation-ships. We have priorities for how we choose to spend our free time. We have priorities at work and in the home. Sometimes, these prior-ities will clash against each other. For example, you might prefer to sleep in each morning, but your boss sets a mandatory meeting at eight o'clock. So, there is tension between your personal priority of rest and your priority of doing well at work. You have to choose which priority will be elevated.

In the long run, each of us will develop one ultimate priority—one ideal or person or desire that trumps everything else. We all have a number-one priority in our lives. So, you need to make an intentional and deliberate choice about that priority. Ideally, you should sit down and evaluate the different areas of your life—the values and desires that are pulling you in different directions—and decide which of those values and desires is most important.

If you don't make that kind of informed decision, you will still have an ultimate priority guiding your life, but you will drift into it based on whatever is most urgent or whatever feels best at a given moment in time. Your priorities will be determined by your habits, which means that you won't have clarity about your life. Instead, you will live in chaos.

3. Do you make deliberate decisions about your priorities, or do you tend to drift between those priorities from moment to moment or season to season? Explain.

4. What do you think is your number-one priority in life right now?

....

....

....

....

....

....

....

....

....

....

....

....

TIME WITH JESUS SHOULD BE YOUR FIRST PRIORITY

So, how do you choose to practice spiritual disciplines and invest in your relationship with God even when it is not necessarily what you *want* to do with your time and resources each day? The answer is not to force yourself and practice the disciplines grudgingly. Rather, the answer is to *adjust* your priorities. Specifically, the way to help yourself engage the practice of spiritual disciplines is to intentionally choose time with Jesus as the number-one priority in your life.

Earlier, we looked at the story of Mary and Martha (see Luke 10:38–42). Now, as we read this story, we need to understand that Mary and Martha (and their brother Lazarus) were dear friends of Jesus. They were a wealthy family, which means they weren't coming to Jesus and looking for Him to give them something all the time. Instead, they simply enjoyed His presence. In turn, Jesus used their home as a place of refuge during His travels.

On this day, the sisters had received word that Jesus was on His way. We can reasonably infer they worked together for hours to prepare for His arrival—and the arrival of His disciples. It was a lot of work, and I am sure that both sisters had been at it for hours by the time Jesus actually arrived. However, when He did arrive, the sisters responded in a different way. Mary immediately stopped what she was doing, and "sat at Jesus' feet" (verse 39). Martha took a different path. She continued all the preparations that were necessary for the evening meal.

Jesus' response to the sisters' different actions is critical, because He revealed what our first priority should be. He said, "Martha, Martha, you are worried and troubled about many things. But one thing is needed, and Mary has chosen that good part" (verses 41–42). One thing is most important. One thing is most urgent. One thing will provide the most value in our lives and the best return on the investment of our time: spending time with Jesus.

When you make that your first priority, everything else will fall into place.

5. What makes you feel especially frazzled or frustrated when it comes to different priorities tugging at your time and attention?

6. What does it look like when spending time with Jesus is the first priority in a person's life? What are the symptoms of that reality?

....

....

....

....

....

....

....

....

....

....

....

....

TIME WITH JESUS IMPROVES YOUR RELATIONSHIP WITH HIM

Intentionally choosing to elevate time with Jesus as the first priority in your life will benefit you in many ways. First, it will bring you to a deeper and more meaningful personal connection to Christ. It will strengthen your faith. You realize that you are friends with God—the Creator and Sustainer of the universe. When you start to understand that God Himself is speaking to you, giving direction, and answering your prayers, you feel the weight of that blessing.

God desires to speak to you. He will make this crystal clear if you only give Him the time. The more you feel that reciprocal connection, the more your faith in Christ will be strengthened. Furthermore, making time with Jesus your first priority will enlarge your view of God. So many people's understanding of God is cramped and confined. They only see or perceive Him inside this little box—a "god" of their own mind. But when you begin to see how He works in your life, and how He is orchestrating situations and circumstances in the future that you cannot even see right now, you begin to get a sense of God's immensity. The more you give time to Jesus, the more you recognize His sovereignty and incredible power.

One thing that certainly will happen when you spend time with Jesus is that He will purify your heart. I believe one of the primary reasons most people don't get along with the Lord is because they don't want to face themselves. They have baggage and sin they do not want to confront. They have frustrations and anxieties and don't believe God can handle them. But He can. He can take every single need you bring before Him.

When you come before God and you say, "Lord, speak to my heart," He doesn't scratch His head to figure out what to say. He knows every single thing that is going on in your heart and mind. He responds by gently showing you a better way: *That's not the right attitude. Shouldn't have said that. You're causing damage when you treat him that way.* Yes, the purification process is sometimes painful, but the purifying work of the Holy Spirit and the presence of your Lord is absolutely precious to any child of God who wants to grow.

7. What benefits have you received from spending time with Jesus?

....

....

....

....

....

....

....

....

....

....

8. When have you gone through seasons where you made God a high priority in your life? What happened?

....

....

....

....

....

....

....

....

....

....

TIME WITH JESUS IMPROVES YOUR LIFE IN GENERAL

Not only will your relationship with God improve when you make spending time with Jesus your number-one priority, but your life in general will also be uplifted. You become a better version of yourself. Your experiences are elevated to a new level.

For instance, you will find that Jesus can quiet your spirit when you feel frustration, agitation, and anxiety. It doesn't matter how stormy your circumstances might be. When you get alone with Jesus, the peace He brings is incredible. This is why David said, "My soul follows close behind you" (Psalm 63:8). God takes away those things that cause agitation in your spirit.

Next, you gain a renewed level of energy. I cannot explain how this works . . . I just know it does work! When you get on your face before the Lord, shut out everything else, begin to listen to Him, and start to express your love and your praise toward Him, there is a divine energy that surges through your human body. I am talking physiologically . . . something happens. You will feel not just recharged but actually *supercharged*.

Finally, you will discover that setting Jesus as the number-one priority in your life will be the greatest time-saver. When you connect with Christ in a meaningful way, you receive wisdom and clarity like you have never imagined. You start to see things closer to God's point of view, which means you gain a sense of what is really important—and what is not. You begin to see which decisions really need to be made and which are silly or unimportant.

So, if you are a believer in Christ, I challenge you to spend time with Jesus and see what happens to your time. He will multiply those moments. He will multiply those minutes. He will multiply those hours. He will multiply those days! Invest in Jesus by making time with Him your number-one priority, and you will reap the benefits for a lifetime.

9. Which of the benefits described above sounds most appealing? Why?

10. What have you learned throughout this study that you are most excited to put into practice?

TODAY AND TOMORROW

Today: I will make spending time with Jesus
my number-one priority.

Tomorrow: I will allow Jesus to transform me and
bless me as I continue to prioritize time with Him.

CLOSING PRAYER

Heavenly Father, we want the best that You have for us. We acknowledge today that the way we can receive Your best is to put You first in everything in our lives. We want to know You, love You, learn from You, and be the people that you have appointed us to be in Your kingdom. We know that You are ready and willing to transform us and enable us to grow. Today, we choose to make pursuing You our life's priority. Thank You, Lord, for Your continual faithfulness to us.

NOTES AND PRAYER REQUESTS

Use this space to write any key points, questions, or prayer requests from this week's study.

LEADER'S GUIDE

Thank you for choosing to lead your group through this Bible study from Dr. Charles F. Stanley on *Practicing Basic Spiritual Disciplines*. The rewards of being a leader are different from those of participating, and it is our prayer that your own walk with Jesus will be deepened by this experience. During the twelve lessons in this study, you will be helping your group members explore and discuss key themes about how they can practice basic spiritual disciplines on a daily basis. There are multiple components in this section that can help you structure your lessons and discussion time, so please be sure to read and consider each one.

BEFORE YOU BEGIN

Before your first meeting, make sure your group members each have a copy of *Practicing Basic Spiritual Disciplines* so they can follow along in the study guide and have their answers written out ahead of time. Alternately, you can hand out the study guides at your first meeting and give the group members some time to look over the material and ask any preliminary questions. During your first meeting, be sure to send a sheet around the room and have the members write down their name, phone number, and email address so you can keep in touch with them during the week.

To ensure everyone has a chance to participate in the discussion, the ideal size for a group is around eight to ten people. If there are more than ten people, break up the bigger group into smaller subgroups. Make sure the members are committed to participating each week, as this will help create stability and help you better prepare the structure of the meeting.

At the beginning of each meeting, you may wish to start the group time by asking the group members to provide their initial reactions to the material they have read during the week. The goal is to just get the group members' preliminary thoughts—so encourage them at this point to keep their answers brief. Ideally, you want everyone in the group to get a chance to share some of their thoughts, so try to keep the responses to a minute or less.

Give the group members a chance to answer, but tell them to feel free to pass if they wish. With the rest of the study, it's generally not a good idea to have everyone answer every question—a free-flowing discussion is more desirable. But with the opening icebreaker questions, you can go around the circle. Encourage shy people to share, but don't force them. Also, try to keep any one person from dominating the discussion so everyone will have the opportunity to participate.

WEEKLY PREPARATION

As the group leader, there are a few things you can do to prepare for each meeting:

- *Be thoroughly familiar with the material in the lesson.* Make sure you understand the content of each lesson so you know how to structure the group time and are prepared to lead the group discussion.

- *Decide, ahead of time, which questions you want to discuss.* Depending on how much time you have each week, you may not be able to reflect on every question. Select specific questions that you feel will evoke the best discussion.

- *Take prayer requests.* At the end of your discussion, take prayer requests from your group members and then pray for one another.

- *Pray for your group.* Pray for your group members throughout the week and ask God to lead them as they study His Word.

- *Bring extra supplies to your meeting.* The members should bring their own pens for writing notes, but it's a good idea to have extras available for those who forget. You may also want to bring paper and additional Bibles.

STRUCTURING THE GROUP DISCUSSION TIME

You will need to determine with your group how long you want to meet each week so you can plan your time accordingly. Generally, most groups like to meet for either sixty minutes or ninety minutes, so you could use one of the following schedules:

SECTION	60 Minutes	90 Minutes
WELCOME (group members arrive and get settled)	5 minutes	10 minutes
ICEBREAKER (group members share their initial thoughts regarding the content in the lesson)	10 minutes	15 minutes
DISCUSSION (discuss the Bible study questions you selected ahead of time)	35 minutes	50 minutes
PRAYER/CLOSING (pray together as a group and dismiss)	10 minutes	15 minutes

As the group leader, it is up to you to keep track of the time and keep things moving according to your schedule. If your group is having a good discussion, don't feel the need to stop and move on to the next question. Remember, the purpose is to pull together ideas and share unique insights on the lesson. Encourage everyone to participate, but don't be concerned if certain group members are more quiet. They may just be internally reflecting on the questions and need time to process their ideas before they can share them.

Group Dynamics

Leading a group study can be a rewarding experience for you and your group members—but that doesn't mean there won't be challenges. Certain members may feel uncomfortable in discussing topics that they consider very personal and might be afraid of being called on. Some members might have disagreements on specific issues. To help prevent these scenarios, consider establishing the following ground rules:

- If someone has a question that may seem off topic, suggest that it is discussed at another time, or ask the group if they are okay with addressing that topic.

- If someone asks a question to which you do not know the answer, confess that you don't know and move on. If you feel comfortable, you can invite the other group members to give their opinions or share their comments based on personal experience.

- If you feel like a couple of people are talking much more than others, direct questions to people who may not have shared yet. You could even ask the more dominating members to help draw out the quiet ones.

- When there is a disagreement, encourage the members to process the matter in love. Invite members from opposing sides to evaluate their opinions and consider the ideas of the other members. Lead the group through Scripture that addresses the topic, and look for common ground.

When issues arise, encourage your group to follow these words from Scripture: "Love one another" (John 13:34), "If it is possible, as much as depends on you, live peaceably with all men" (Romans 12:18), "Whatever things are true . . . noble . . . pure . . . lovely . . . if there is any virtue and if there is anything praiseworthy—meditate on these things" (Philippians 4:8), and "Be swift to hear, slow to speak, slow to wrath" (James 1:19). This will make your group time more rewarding and beneficial for everyone who attends.

Thank you again for your willingness to lead your group. May God reward your efforts and dedication, equip you to guide your group in the weeks ahead, and make your time together in *Practicing Basic Spiritual Disciplines* fruitful for His kingdom.

Also Available from Charles F. Stanley

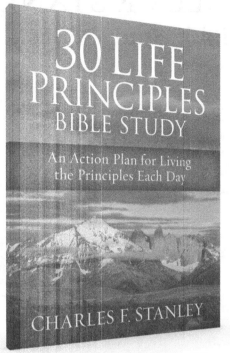

9780310082521   Softcover

30 LIFE PRINCIPLES BIBLE STUDY

An Action Plan for Living the Principles Each Day

During his many years of ministry, Dr. Charles Stanley has faithfully highlighted the 30 life principles that have guided him and helped him to grow in his knowledge, service, and love of God. In this Bible study, you will explore each of these principles in depth and learn how to make them a part of your everyday life. As you do, you will find yourself growing in your relationship with Christ and on the road to the future God has planned for you.

Available now at your favorite bookstore.

THOMAS NELSON
Since 1798

Also Available in the
CHARLES F. STANLEY
Bible Study Series

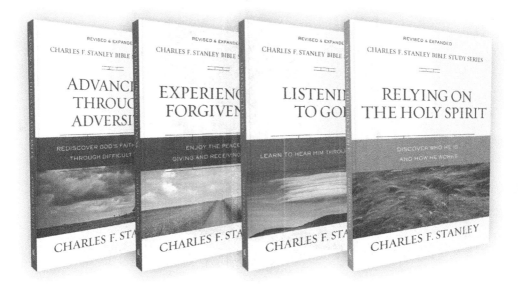

Each study draws on Dr. Stanley's many years of
teaching the guiding principles found in God's Word,
showing how we can apply them in practical ways to
every situation we face. This edition of the series has
been completely revised and updated, and includes
two brand-new lessons from Dr. Stanley.

Available now at your favorite bookstore.
More volumes coming soon.

The Charles F. Stanley Bible Study Series is a unique
approach to Bible study, incorporating biblical truth,
personal insights, emotional responses,
and a call to action.

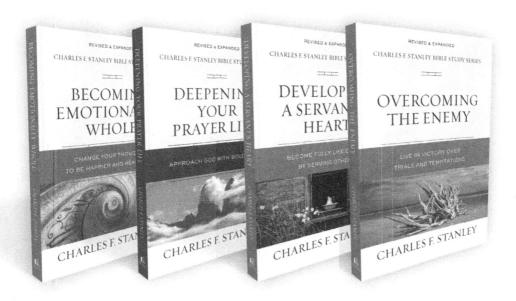

THOMAS NELSON
Since 1798